FAMILY LAW BOOT CAMP:

The Essential Guide to Representing Yourself in a Colorado Family Law Case

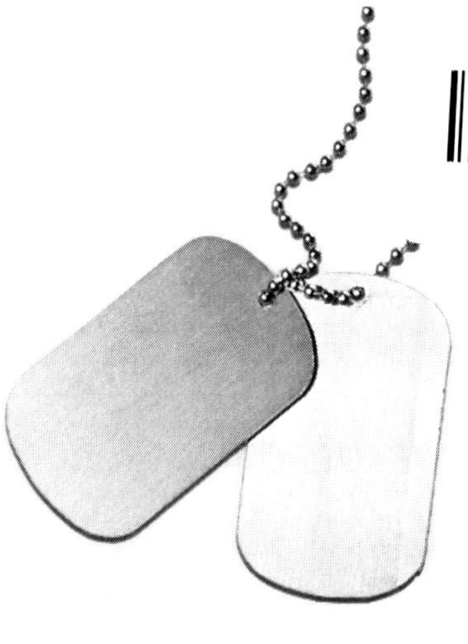

US Army Veteran and Family Law Attorney

Alisha Taibo Coombe

ISBN: 978-1-7359748-7-3

The Unapologetic Voice House
Scottsdale, AZ

www.theunapologeticvoicehouse.com

for Dan, Johnny, Emma, Sophia and Olivia, who make me the happiest wife, mommy and step-mom in the world.

CONTENTS

ACKNOWLEDGEMENTS

My deepest gratitude goes first to the love of my life, Dan Coombe. Without a husband like you, it would have been impossible to write a book while being a full-time working mom. You make marriage easy and life fun every day. Thank you for always encouraging and supporting me, giving me your time, reviewing and editing the book, and offering positive and objective feedback. You are my best friend and soulmate. I love you forever. SWNGBGR!

The completion of this book would not have been possible without the assistance and feedback of my mentor and dear friend, Judge Don Toussaint. Thank you for giving the most valuable gift a person can give - your time - to mentoring me and reviewing and editing this book. I truly appreciate your kindness, encouragement and friendship.

PROLOGUE

It may interest you to know that 75% of all family law cases in Colorado courts are filed by people who are representing themselves. That's an incredible number. That means you are in good company, and you are not alone. At $250 an hour and up, legal services have become a luxury most people cannot afford. However, the Courts maintain that parties who represent themselves without a lawyer are held to the same standards as attorneys. While this book cannot replace three years of law school, it can provide you with the information and tools you need to effectively represent yourself in your family law case.

This book will help you better prepare your case by guiding you to the law the judge will apply, orient you to the process, and tell you what you need to do, in what order, and what the court expects of you in terms of deadlines, forms, presentation and demeanor. This book was written from the perspective of going through a Colorado family law case from start to finish, and the timelines and rules pertain specifically to Colorado. I have tried to touch on the major points of a family law case, such as division of assets and debts, support payments, and custody, as well as some lesser common cases like adoption and contempt.

This book is not legal advice. Legal advice refers to when an attorney tells you what you should do in your specific case. I do not know you and cannot possibly give you legal advice concerning your unique situation. If you have specific questions about what you should do at any given moment in your specific case, you should consult with an attorney. There are attorneys who are willing to help you by meeting with you on a one-time consultation basis, and who are willing to advise on an ongoing basis without expensive retainers or entering their appearance as your counsel in your case. This limited type of representation is also known as "unbundled services" and a Google search for "unbundled services attorney" and your geographic area will reveal attorneys who offer these services.

With the help of this book, you will gain a better understanding of the process of a family law case. You will learn how to draft motions effectively, understand the timeframes involved in your case, how to interpret contract language and how to prepare for trial. This book contains helpful hints during all phases of your case and a summary of the laws you may need to cite or refer to. You will learn how to organize a case for trial, select witnesses, and present evidence.

This book can't replace hiring an attorney, but it can teach you the tactics and basic skills needed to litigate a case on your own by providing you with the information and resources you will need to present your case like a pro.

A TO Z GUIDE OF HELPFUL LEGAL TERMS

Learning the law can feel like learning a different language. Below is an alphabetical glossary of many legal terms you may encounter in your family law case. As you read this book, refer back to this guide as a quick reference tool to help you understand every step of the process.

A

- **Alimony.** See Maintenance.
- **APR.** Allocation of Parental Rights. In Colorado, this is the legal term for a child custody case.
- **Applicable law.** Family laws, also called domestic laws, are State laws, not Federal laws. That means that family laws typically differ from state to state. When you're researching laws, research state laws in Colorado. If you can't find Colorado case law that supports your position, but you can find another State's case law that does, you can use it to try and persuade the Court of your position, but the Court is not required to follow it.
- **Arbitration** - A method of dispute resolution where parties engage in negotiation with the assistance of a third-party neutral, called an arbitrator, whose decision is binding.

B

- **Black's Law Dictionary.** If you're going to represent yourself, you may just want to buy one of these. You will be looking up a lot of words during this process.

C

- **Caption.** The introductory part of a court document or document to be filed with the court stating the jurisdiction, names of the parties, type of case, name of person filing the document, case number, courtroom where assigned, and relief requested.

- **Case law** refers to appellate-level cases interpreting statutes (the law created by our Legislature). You can find cases interpreting statutes at the end of each statute. If you get a Colorado Revised Statute book and look at the end of each section, you will see case law summaries. You can also find these online. Links to helpful resources to research case law are provided in the Appendix.
- **Case Management Order.** A document you get from the court at the beginning of your case that states all the deadlines for your case and all the required steps to get to the end of your case.
- **Child Support.** This refers to periodic (typically monthly) payments a court may order a spouse to pay the other spouse to assist with support of the children. The purpose of child support is to equalize the income coming into both households for the benefit of the children, so the children feel they have the same resources at both homes.
- **C.R.C.P. Colorado Rules of Civil Procedure.** Court rules that are drafted and approved by the Colorado Supreme Court and govern the process by which cases proceed in Colorado.
- **C.R.S. Colorado Revised Statutes.** These are the Colorado laws passed by the State Legislature.

D

- **Decree.** Another name for a final order in a family law case.
- Designation of the Parties: In Colorado, parties to a domestic case are designated the Petitioner and Respondent (instead of plaintiff and defendant). The person filing the case is the Petitioner. The person responding is the Respondent. Family law

cases are also called Domestic Relations cases.

- **Disclosures.** Documents both sides are required to exchange at the start of the case.
- **Discovery.** Requests for additional information from one party to the other after disclosures have been completed.
- **Division.** The Courtroom number.
- **Docket.** The court's open case list.
- **Domestic Relations.** Another term for "family law." Abbreviated "DR" in a family law case.

E

- **Evidence.** You need some. You can't just come to court and argue your ex owes you money without showing receipts for the amount and maybe some emails to him where you tried to collect. Think about what you have that supports your case other than your own testimony and bring it (documents, witnesses, or both). This is especially important if you are prosecuting a contempt where your burden of proof is the tough "beyond a reasonable doubt." That means you better come to court with some good evidence and know the rules of how to get it admitted.
- **Exhibits.** Before the Court can look at your evidence, you must label it as Exhibits. Petitioner's exhibits are numbered, Respondent's exhibits are letters.

F

- **Fact Finder.** The judge is also known as the Fact Finder because her job is to decide who is telling the truth where there are conflicting stories, and then determine what is fair and equitable in financial matters, and in the best interests of the child in custody matters. What you believe is fair may not be what the judge believes is fair, and you know it will differ from what your ex thinks is fair. The best thing you can do to bolster your credibility is tell the truth.

- **Filing** – The act of submitting a document to the Court for processing and action.

G

- **Gamble.** That's what a trial is. You're betting on half your stuff that the judge will see things your way. It is really, really, REALLY rare for a party to get everything he/she wants at trial. You have a better chance of getting struck by lightning in a house you bought with your lottery winnings. Keep that in mind when you're in settlement negotiations and don't get **Greedy**.
- **Garnish.** The act of intercepting a party's wages to pay child support or maintenance.

H

- **Hearings** are trials, and trials are hearings in domestic court. They're synonymous.

I

- **Initial Status Conference.** Meeting between the parties and the Court at the beginning of the case where the parties are told the deadlines in their case and other requirements.
- **Injunction.** A court order commanding you to do to something or prohibiting you from doing something.
- **Internet Research.** Unsurprisingly, the internet is a helpful tool in researching law. There is a plethora of free resources available to you. Web addresses to these are provided in the Appendix.

J

- **JTMC.** Joint Trial Management Certificate. This is a document you file typically 7-14 days before trial that tells the Court the case stipulations, undisputed facts, requests for attorney fees, disputed issues, specific points of law you are relying on, lists of your witnesses, and list of exhibits.
- **Jeans**. Don't wear these to court. Or shorts, or sweats, or a skimpy tank top, or clothes with dirty words printed on them, or Julia Roberts' boots from Pretty Woman. If your mother would shake her head in disappointment looking at what you are wearing to court, change clothes. Look respectable for the person who is about to decide your fate, for Pete's sake!

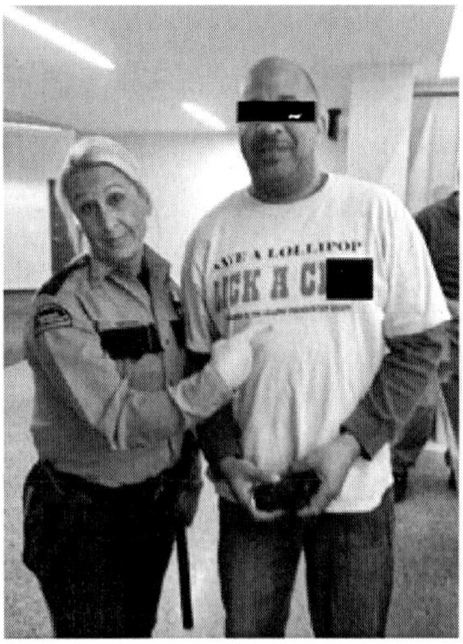

This is an actual picture I took at Court in the security line in 2013. Don't be this guy.

- **Judge**. A person who is appointed by the Governor to hear and resolve legal disputes people bring to Court. Judges are also known as "**Judicial Officers**."

- **Judgment**. Another word for a court's ruling.
- **Jurisdiction**. The Court's authority to hear a case.

K

- If you're embarking on a custody battle, you may be tempted to **kidnap** the kids and take them to another state. Don't. If you do this, you can **kiss** your custody chances goodbye.

L

- **Latin**. Lawyers Love Latin. The first Latin word you need to know is *Pro se* (pronounced pro say), which is Latin for "self-represented." So, if you're representing yourself, you are a *pro se* party. You are appearing in court *pro se*. Latin words are always italicized, and you'll see them regularly in cases.
- **Litigation** – The process of carrying on the case between the filing of the case and resolution.

M

- **Magistrate**. A Magistrate is like a judge in that this person hears and resolves legal disputes and is considered a "Judicial Officer." However, a Magistrate differs from a judge mainly in that 1) they are hired by the Court rather than appointed by the Governor 2) they have fewer powers than a judge. The differences are covered more in depth in Chapter 1 under Magistrates and Judges.
- **Maintenance**. This is the word the Court uses instead of alimony or spousal support. This refers to periodic (typically monthly) payments a court may order a higher income earning spouse to pay the other spouse in a divorce. This is different

from child support. Maintenance is not ordered in every case. The purpose is to financially assist a lower income earning spouse for a period until they can become more self-sufficient following a divorce.

- **Marital Property**. Property that was acquired by either party during the marriage even if it is not titled in both names (with some exceptions). To determine whether your property is marital or pre-marital, consult with § 14-10-113, C.R.S.
- **Maybe**. The answer to every legal question. Usually, laws are not as black and white as "you must be 35 years old to run for President." The general answer to the question, "can I do this under the law?" is "maybe." Especially in family law and especially when it comes to custody. The judge has the ultimate discretion to decide what's in the best interests of the child and what's equitable in dividing stuff and determining maintenance. This is why lawyers have jobs.
- **Mediation.** A method of dispute resolution where parties engage in negotiation with the assistance of a third-party neutral, called a mediator, who assists the parties in finding solutions, but cannot make binding decisions regarding resolution of the case.
- **Modify**. Lawyers use this word instead of "change." For example, you would file a motion to modify child support (rather than a motion to change child support).
- **Motion**. A captioned document that a party files asking the court to do something.
- **Motions hearing**. The final hearing where the court will rule on the requested modification of orders.

N

- **Nervous**. You should be nervous going to court. If you're not nervous, you're not taking it seriously. You will be less nervous though if you plan your trial in advance! And expect something to surprise you. Something surprises me every time I go to court. Some witness will say something you weren't expecting, or the judge will rule on an objection in a way that makes you question his lucidity. Still, the better prepared you are, the less surprises you will see and the more confident you will feel.

O

- **Overruled.** You will learn how to make objections and what to object to in this book. When the judge does NOT agree with your objection, it will be **Overruled.** When she does agree with it, it will be **Sustained**. (I remembered this as a law student by changing the word sustained to YESstained in my head and remembering Overruled was NOverruled.)

P

- **Permanent orders**. Refers to the final order issued in a case.
- **Permanent orders hearing**. The final hearing where the court will decide final orders in a new case.
- **Petition.** A form that a party drafts and files with the Court to start a new case.
- **Plan Plan Plan**! Plan your case using the trial plan in this book. Don't show up to Court thinking you're going to just tell the judge your side of the story and she'll see things your way. You need to prepare your evidence, witnesses, and presentation of your case in order to convey your side of the story and why you win under the law, as effectively as possible.
- **Possession, custody and control**. When you exchange disclosures or discovery, you are required to produce documentation that is in your "possession, custody, or control" meaning even if you do not have a copy, you are required to request one

if you have the authority to do so.

- **Post-decree.** A case filed by a party requesting to modify existing orders.
- **Pre-decree.** A new case that has never had final orders issued.
- **Produce**. Legal word for "give." In the law, we request parties to "produce" documents meaning we are requesting that they give us a copy of a document they have.
- ***Pro Se.*** Latin word meaning a person who is representing him/herself in a court case. If you do not have a lawyer representing you, you are *pro se*.
- **Protection Order**. Also called a "restraining order." An order prohibiting one party (the restrained party) from contacting the other party (the protected party).

Q

- **QDRO**. **Qualified Domestic Relations Order**. A document that tells the retirement plan administrator that you got divorced, and that the party who did not originally own the retirement plan was awarded some portion of the asset. If you're getting a divorce and dividing a retirement asset, you will divide it using a QDRO which allows you to transfer the funds to an account in the other spouse's name without any tax consequence, while retaining the retirement asset status.

R

- **Respect**. Show respect to everyone in the courtroom, even if you secretly wish you could make them dead with your eyes. Good courtroom demeanor will add credibility to you as a witness. Remember to stand every time you talk to the judge, even if the other party or lawyer is not. Unless the judge tells you that you don't have to, do it. No one has ever been faulted in court for being too respectful.

S

- **Service of Process**. The act of providing the other party with the papers being filed with the Court.
- **Spousal Support.** See Maintenance.
- **Statutes** are the laws created by the Colorado Legislature. Colorado Revised Statutes is what Colorado laws are called.
- **Stipulation.** Any agreements reached during the case between you and the other party.
- **Subpoena.** A form issued by the Court requiring someone to either appear in court or produce documentation.
- **Sustained.** You will learn how to make objections and what to object to in this book. When the judge does NOT agree with your objection, it will be **Overruled.** When she does agree with it, it will be **Sustained**. (I remembered this as a law student by changing the word sustained to YESstained in my head and remembering Overruled was NOverruled.)
- **§**. No, this is not Prince's alter ego. This symbol is read as "section." We cite to the Colorado Revised Statutes as § 14-10-101 (for example). You would read this as "Section fourteen ten one oh one" and the court would know what you mean. Or, you could say "Section fourteen dash ten dash one oh one."

T

- **Temporary Orders**. Interim orders that are only in effect until permanent orders are issued.
- **Temporary Orders Hearing.** A hearing that occurs while litigation is pending to determine interim orders concerning custody, family support, payments of debts and other matters de-

manding immediate attention.

- **TMC (**Trial Management Certificate). This is a document you file typically 7-14 days before trial that tells the Court the case stipulations (agreements between you and the other side), undisputed facts, requests for attorney fees, disputed issues, specific points of law you are relying on, lists of your witnesses, and list of exhibits.
- **Timing.** If you miss court deadlines, your case could be dismissed, meaning you lose that $200 filing fee and must start all over again. Read your case management order, which contains all the deadlines in your case and forms you need to submit to ensure your case moves along the way it is supposed to.

U

- **Undisputed facts**. These are facts that neither you nor your opponent disagree on. These are gold to you - even the bad ones because you need to anticipate the facts that will be used against you.

V

- **Valuation**. If you or your ex have real estate, a business, an antique coin collection or the like, you may need to have this valued as part of your divorce.
- **Venue**. The county where the case is heard.

W

- **Wage Garnishment**. This is also called an Income Assignment and refers to your wages being garnished to pay child support or maintenance.

X

- Expect **X-rated** evidence to be used against you. I recommend avoiding texting naked pictures of yourself during your case. Usually this dirty tactic is useless as it has no relevance to your case, but if you were taking sexy pictures of yourself in a dressing room with your child right there and posting those on Instagram, expect that to come up.

Y

- **Your Honor**. This is what you call the judge. Not Sir or Ma'am. Always **Your Honor**.

Z

- You will wish you were divorcing Mark **Zuckerberg**. At least you have this super helpful book!

SECTION 1 – STARTING YOUR CASE

I served in the United States Army from 1994 to 1998. Before I went off to Army basic training (also known as "boot camp"), my grandpa gave me this advice: "Keep your mouth shut and don't volunteer for nuthin." Sounds wise, although looking back, volunteering actually got me out of a lot of cruddy detail in Boot Camp. My advice to somebody about to go into Army basic training is the same as I'd give someone about to embark on a difficult case.

1) Keep your focus on the end goal. This is one of the toughest things you'll ever go through in your life, but it is temporary. Get in, do what's required, and always keep an eye on the light at the end of the tunnel knowing that if you work hard, keep your head up, and maintain professionalism and good attitude, you will get through this successfully.

2) Prepare before you go. In the Army, you don't start doing push-ups after you get there. You learn how to do your push-ups before you go. You got this book- you're ahead of the game! Now read it, learn the law, learn how to prepare your case, and know what to expect before it happens as much as you can.

3) Get a good battle buddy. You are going to need that friend who never gets tired of listening to you. One who will sit down with you on tough nights or go run with you, and who will be with you through it all. I cannot stress the importance of a good battle buddy. (Shout out to my girl Christina Oxier!)

CHAPTER 1: OVERVIEW OF A FAMILY LAW CASE

Family Law cases are also known as Domestic Relations cases, so you may hear it both ways. These cases are divided into two types of cases: pre-decree or post-decree cases. A pre-decree case refers to a brand-new case that has just been filed, such as a new divorce case or a new custody case. Pre-decree refers to the fact that no orders have ever been issued regarding this specific custody matter or divorce matter – thus it is pre (before) decree (final orders). A post-decree case refers to a case that is before the court on the request of one party to *modify* existing orders (decree). Thus, it is post (after) decree (final orders). Your case will either be a pre-decree or a post-decree case.

Court cases are governed by a set of rules called the Colorado Rules of Civil Procedure (abbreviated as C.R.C.P.). This book tells you timeframes for court cases, the schedule the court expects you to follow, and even what documents are required and what information you are entitled to. This book provides you with the timelines and requirements you need to know and will tell you which rule governs so you can look it up yourself if you wish.

Below is a snapshot of the process of a Pre-Decree and a Post-Decree case. Do not be concerned if you are unsure of what some of these things mean. This book will cover every step.

Pre-Decree Case Process

- Draft Petition, Case Information Sheet, and Summons
- File Petition and Case Information Sheet with the Court. Have

clerk sign summons, stamp your copies.

- Get Case Management Order
- Have opposing party personally served by process server with Petition, Case Information Sheet and Summons and Case Management Order.
- Attend Initial Status Conference
- Exchange disclosures
- Engage in discovery (optional).
- Possibly go to Temporary Orders Hearing
- Go to mediation. If you resolve case in mediation, file agreement and all final proposed orders with the court and you're done.
- Go to Permanent Orders Hearing if mediation is unsuccessful.

Post-Decree case Process

- Draft Motion
- File Motion with the Court. Have clerk stamp your copies.
- Get Case Management Order
- Serve opposing party (typically by mail).
- Possibly attend initial status conference (depends on jurisdiction)
- Engage in disclosures (if motion is for purpose of modifying something financial)
- Engage in discovery (optional).
- Go to mediation. If you resolve case in mediation, file agreement and any final proposed orders with the court and you're done.
- Go to Motions Hearing if mediation is unsuccessful.

In family law cases, the main rule you need to know is C.R.C.P. 16.2. That rule provides the general process for both pre- and post-decree matters. Chapter 3 will outline exactly what deadlines you need to be aware of based on the rules that apply to your type of case.

HOW TO START YOUR CASE

If you are starting a new domestic relations case, you will start with three forms: a petition, a case information sheet, and you will also need to give the clerk a summons to sign for you, (which tells the person when and where to appear or respond in court). In addition, you need to prepare either a waiver of service or return of service – these are the forms that tell the Court how the other party was served with the initial paperwork. If you think the other side will accept the papers you are filing and agree to participate in the case, you can ask them to sign a waiver of service. If not, and you need to have the person served, you will give your process server the return of service to fill out once service is complete.

If you are filing a motion to modify (or change) existing orders, you just need to file the motion asking the court to do what you want. Since the court already has authority over the other party from when it entered the original decree, you can "serve" the other party by mailing them a copy of the motion you filed.

Court forms in Colorado are sometimes referred to as "JDF" forms because of the form number they are assigned. For example, a Petition for Dissolution of Marriage is a JDF 1101. I will refer you to JDF forms in this book from time to time.

Court Forms can be downloaded from the Court's website at:

https://www.courts.state.co.us/Forms/

"Filing" these documents refers to the process of delivering the documents to the main clerk's office at the courthouse in the county you want the case heard. Generally, people are required to file their cases in the county in which one of them lives. When you file your case, you should make copies of all the documents you are filing and ask the clerk to stamp your copy. The clerk will date-stamp your copies so you will have proof of when you filed the paperwork. The clerks do a fantastic job but they're only human, and it is possible for things to get lost. By keeping a stamped copy for yourself, you will be able to prove when you filed something should a mistake ever happen.

To file a Family Law case, here is a brief list of what you need to file:

Divorce or Legal Separation with or without children
Petition for Dissolution of Marriage (JDF 1101), Summons (JDF 1102), Case Information Sheet (JDF 1000)

Annulment
FILE: Petition for Declaration of Invalidity of Marriage (JDF 1601), Summons (JDF 1602), Case Information Sheet (JDF 1000)

New Custody

Petition for Allocation of Parental Rights and Responsibilities (JDF 1413), Summons (JDF 1102), Case Information Sheet (JDF 1000)

Stepparent Adoption

Petition for Stepparent Adoption (JDF 501), Petition to Terminate Parental Rights (JDF 520), Affidavit of Abandonment (JDF 525), Affidavit of Diligent Efforts (JDF 526), Consent to Adoption (by custodial parent) (JDF 509), Statement of Fees (JDF 454), Notice of Adoption Proceeding and Summons to Respond (JDF 506), Notice of Hearing (JDF 514), Proposed Finding of Fact and Decree Pursuant to § 19-5-203 (JDF 521), Proposed Final Adoption Decree (JDF 521),

CBI Background check, retrievable here: https://www.colorado.gov/pacific/cbi/employment-background-checks

FBI background check, retrievable here: https://www.fbi.gov/services/cjis/compact-council/national-fingerprint-based-background-checks-steps-for-success.

DHS background check, retrievable here:

http://coloradoofficeofearlychildhood.force.com/oec/OEC_Providers?p=Providers&s=Background-Checks&lang=en.

Vital Records Report of Adoption, retrievable here:
https://www.colorado.gov/pacific/sites/default/files/CHEIS_VR_Form_Adoption_Report-of-Adoption-Form_0916_1.pdf

Contempt
Motion for Citation for Contempt and Proposed Citation (JDF 1816), Order to Issue Citation and Citation to Show Cause (JDF 1817)

Motion to Modify [anything]
Motion to Modify [Child Support] (JDF 1403); [Maintenance] (JDF 1401; [Allocation of Parental Responsibilities] (JDF 1406)

New Child Support Case
Petition for Allocation of Parental Rights and Responsibilities (JDF 1413), Summons (JDF 1102), Case Information Sheet (JDF 1000)

Motion to Restrict Parenting Time
Motion to Restrict Parenting Time (JDF 1406)

Protection Order

Verified Complaint for Protection Order (JDF 402), Affidavit regarding Children (JDF 404), Incident Checklist (JDF 401), Temporary Protection Order (JDF 398), Permanent Protection Order (JDF 399).

This is not an exhaustive list and only covers the main types of family law cases. For example, in a stepparent adoption, I listed the forms with the assumption that the other parent abandoned. However, you may have a case where the other parent consents to the adoption. This will require that parent also sign a consent form but will not require you file an affidavit of diligent efforts.

To find the forms for the Petitions or Motions you need, visit the Colorado Court website, http://www.courts.state.co.us/. Click on Self Help/Forms, and you'll see a link to Family Law, Adoption, Protection Orders, and all other court forms that are available for free download. This website has instructions on what to file to start your case. This book is not going to repeat that since it is publicly available. The purpose of this book is to help you with your case after you have filed the initial paperwork.

TIP - you do not need a Summons for modifications of existing orders. This is only for starting a new case.

THE CASE CAPTION

Legal documents that are filed with the court must have a caption. A caption tells the court what case the document pertains to, who filed it, the parties' names, the case number, and the court, and whether the party is represented by counsel. Throughout this book, I will refer to captions and captioned documents. A captioned document is a document you file with the court such as a motion or a pleading, that has a caption on it.

A caption in a divorce case looks like this:

<table>
<tr><td>DISTRICT COURT, ARAPAHOE COUNTY, COLORADO
7325 S. Potomac Street
Centennial, Colorado 80112</td><td rowspan="2">

▲ COURT USE ONLY</td></tr>
<tr><td>In re the Marriage of:
BRAD SCHMITT Petitioner,

and

JENNIFER ANDERSON Respondent.</td></tr>
<tr><td>Petitioner, pro se
Brad Schmitt
456 Bellagio Court
Denver, CO 80126
Phone Number: (303) 555-1500
Email: oceans150mm@fitemail.com</td><td>Case Number:
2020 DR 11

Division/Courtroom: 12</td></tr>
<tr><td colspan="2">MOTION TO MODIFY CHILD SUPPORT</td></tr>
</table>

In the caption above, first you see the Court location. This Court is in Arapahoe County, and the caption contains the full address where you can mail or deliver legal documents to be filed. Under that, we have the case type and party names. Because this is a divorce, the case type is an "In re the Marriage of." "In re" is Latin for "in the matter of." Under that the parties' names appear alongside their party designation. Here, Brad is the Petitioner because he was the Petitioner for divorce when the case was filed. In other words, he started the case. Brad will always be listed as the Petitioner in every motion or pleading filed in this case from now on. (That can be confusing to some people. It would seem like whoever is filing a motion with the court should become the Petitioner, but that is not so.)

Under the names in the third box down is the contact information for the party who is filing that document. In this case, Brad is the person filing the motion, so he lists his information in that box. He states he is the Petitioner; he is *pro se* (representing himself); and he states his name, address, phone number, and email. Email is not required here. This is where you state all the ways in which you are willing to accept service in this matter. Here, Brad is willing to accept service of documents by U.S. mail to his address and by email.

To the right of Brad's contact information is the case information. Here, Brad lists his case number and the courtroom or division his case is assigned to. If you do not know the courtroom or division, you can leave it blank. This is helpful to the Court clerks when you file your case to route it to the right judge, but if you don't know, they can look it up. You must put the case number though. If you do not know it, a simple phone call to the Court should help.

The case number consists of three parts: The year the case was first initiated, the type of case, and the sequence number. Here, the year is 2020, meaning the divorce was first filed in 2020. The type of case is a DR case, which is an abbreviation for "Domestic Relations." The sequence number is 11, which means it was the eleventh case filed that year. When you first file a new Petition, you will not have a case number. When you file your Petition, the Court clerk will give you a case number.

Underneath the contact information and court information is the title of the document you are filing. In this case, Brad is filing a Motion to Modify Child Support. Every caption must contain a title.

Note: If you are filing in a custody case (called an APR case, or Allocation of Parental Responsibilities), the case type will be "In re the Interest of," and will contain your child's initials. The Courts have a policy against using children's names in captions for privacy purposes. Here is what that will look like for you:

<table>
<tr><td>In re the Interest of:
S.J.P.

and concerning
BRAD SCHMITT Petitioner,

and

ANGELINA POLI Respondent.</td><td></td></tr>
</table>

Here, their child is listed at the top, and the parents are listed under the "and concerning" line.

In a stepparent adoption case, you are filing two petitions: A Petition for Stepparent Adoption and a Petition for Termination of Parental Rights. In a stepparent adoption, the person wanting to adopt is the Petitioner, and the biological parent they are seeking to terminate is the Respondent.

the Matter of the Petition of: **TTHEW HAMMOND** *the Adoption of a Child* **P.** *Child,* *Concerning* **AD SCHMITT** *ondent*	

Here, Matthew Hammond has filed to adopt S.J.P. and terminate Brad's parental rights.

If you're filing a protection order case against the person you have a divorce case against, and you're filing in the county where you got divorced, then you should file your protection order paperwork under that case number and using that case caption information. If you are seeking the protection order on behalf of your child against the other parent and you already have an existing case concerning the custody of that child, file the protection order under that case number and using that case caption. If you are filing a protection order case against someone with whom you do not have an existing case, or in a county where you did not have an existing domestic relations case with that person, you will be filing a new case and thus you will be the Petitioner and not have a case number.

PARTIES

There are usually two parties to a domestic relations case: the two spouses, or if never married, the two parents. These two parties fill the role of the Petitioner and a Respondent. The Petitioner is the person who initiated the pre-decree case. The Respondent is the person who was served. Sometimes the Respondent is called the Co-Petitioner – this happens if the parties file a Co-Petition, rather than one person filing the Petition and having the other person served. A Co-Petition means the parties both signed the Petition to start the case.

I say that a case *usually* has two parties because sometimes there can be a third (or more) party. This happens when a non-parent, such as grandparents, intervene in a custody case seeking parenting time of a child. The person intervening in the case is called an Intervenor. This can also happen if there are two presumptive fathers in a paternity case. The two fathers may both be named as Respondents, or a presumptive Father may intervene in a case already in progress as an Intervenor. Here is what an Intervenor caption would look like:

<table>
<tr><td>TRICT COURT, ARAPAHOE COUNTY, COLORADO
5 S. Potomac Street
tennial, Colorado 80112</td><td rowspan="2">▲ COURT USE ONLY ▲</td></tr>
<tr><td>e the Interest of:
.

concerning
RONICA KELLER Petitioner,

ANDLER PING Respondent.

EY SCRIBIANI Intervenor.</td></tr>
<tr><td>ervenor, pro se
y Scribiani
Bedford St
tle Rock, CO 80126
ne Number: (303) 555-1014
ail: friends4ever@coffeemail.com</td><td>Case Number:
2020 DR 5

Division/Courtroom: 20</td></tr>
<tr><td colspan="2">MOTION TO SET HEARING</td></tr>
</table>

MAGISTRATES AND JUDGES

You probably already know what a Judge is: the person in the black robe who sits upon an elevated bench and hears cases brought into Court. However, you might not know that your case may be assigned to a Magistrate's courtroom rather than a Judge's Courtroom. It is important to know the difference because you get to choose whether your case stays with the Magistrate or not.

A Judge is appointed by the Governor to hear and decide cases brought into Court. We call this "presiding over" a case. The Judge's job is to be a referee and resolve disputes in trials. Because family law cases are never jury trials, the Judge will be the person who decides everything about the case – whether someone is telling the truth, who seems more credible, objections, how to divide property, custody, and so on. After a judge is appointed by the Governor, they serve for two years and then their name is placed on the ballot in that district for voters to determine whether the judge should be "retained" (stay in that job). District Court Judges then appear on the ballot every six years.

In family law cases, Magistrates perform all of the same functions as judges and are also addressed as "Your Honor." They wear a black robe, sit on an elevated bench and resolve disputes in trials. Many family law cases filed by *pro se* parties are assigned to "Magistrate divisions" (which just means a courtroom where a Magistrate presides). Magistrates are Court employees – not public officials appointed by the Governor. They are hired by the Chief Judge and they can be fired.

So, what is the difference? Magistrates must have the consent of both parties to preside over trials which result in permanent orders concerning property division, maintenance, child support, and custody. What this means to you is if you file a new case for divorce or custody or both and your case is assigned to a Magistrate division, you have a right to object to the case being assigned to a Magistrate division and have the case moved to a Judge's division.

Why would you do this? Well, for one, maybe you've heard things about this Magistrate that you don't like and you think a Judge will be more favorable to you. Maybe you think your case is too complex for the Magistrate and the Judge will have the proper expertise to deal with it. Some Magistrate divisions will not allow parties to set trials for longer than a half-day or a full day. If you believe your case is complex and may require a multi-day trial, you will want to object to the Magistrate's authority. The right to object to the Magistrate is a tool you can use to try and shop for what you perceive as a more favorable judicial officer.

The Deadline to object is either 1) at the time you receive notice your case was assigned to the Magistrate if you are actually standing in Court when you get the notice OR 2) Within 7 days after you receive the written notice. If you miss these deadlines, you cannot object.

One benefit of sticking with the Magistrate is the simpler (and thus, far less expensive) appeal process if you end up with orders you do not agree with. Magistrate orders are appealed to the District Court Judge. The appellate brief is due in 14 days if you are present when the final order is handed out in Court, or in 21 days if the final order is mailed to you. The appellate brief, called a Petition for Magistrate Review, is filed in the same format as you would file a motion. You should file the transcript of the hearing with it and if you don't have it, you should order it and ask for an extension of time to file the Petition for Magistrate Review.

Judges orders, on the other hand, are appealed to the Colorado Court of Appeals. The requirements of the briefs and the deadlines are more complex and much stricter. I highly recommend hiring an attorney if you decide to appeal your case. Appellate practice is very specialized and too complicated to summarize in this book.

Magistrate functions are governed by the Colorado Rules of

Magistrates (C.R.M.) which can be found inside a Colorado Court Rules book at your local law library. The rule governing Petitions for Magistrate Review can be found under C.R.M. Rule 7.

SERVING THE PAPERS

If you have filed a motion in an existing case, and it is not a contempt or protection order motion, then you can serve the other party by mailing the documents to them. You do not need to send them by certified mail. Regular mail is fine. If you are starting a new case, filing a protection order, or filing a contempt motion, you must have the other party personally served.

"Personal service" refers to the process of having the paperwork handed to the other side by someone who is not you. This can be done through the sheriff's department, a professional private process server, or anyone over 18 years of age who is not a party to the case. If the person will be easy to find (say, working a day job at a specific location Monday through Friday), I recommend using the sheriff's department. If the person may be difficult to track down or attempt to avoid services, I recommend a professional process server. They are experts at staking people out to get the job done.

You will give your process server the documents you filed with the court with the summons and the return of service. Make sure to keep a copy of everything for yourself.

If you have no idea where the other party is, you may need to serve them by publication. This means you can put a notice in a newspaper and the court will hang up a sign at the courthouse notifying the opposing party that you have filed this case against him. This practice dates back to the days when our country consisted of a few colonies and people got their news from newspapers and actually reading bulletins posted at the courthouse. Despite the internet having been invented by Al Gore in the 90s, our Legislature has not yet updated this law to allow for service by Facebook, even though it would be more efficient and effective.

Before you can serve by publication, you must get permission from the Court by filing a motion to serve by publication. Before asking for permission, you must try and find the person, and you will have to explain to the court the efforts you made. If the court does not believe you made a diligent enough effort, it may deny your request to serve by publication, so do really try to find the person. If you still can't find the person, you can file a Motion for Publication of Summons or Service by Certified Mail or Publication by Consolidated Notice (JDF Forms 1301 and 1302).

The rules governing service of process can be found at C.R.C.P. Rules 4 and 5.

THE MANDATORY INJUNCTION

The very second you file your divorce or legal separation case, a mandatory injunction automatically goes into effect over you, prohibiting you from doing certain bad things to the opposing party. Likewise, as soon as the opposing party is served with the paperwork, the injunction prohibits them as well from the same bad acts.

The injunction prohibits both parties from hiding or wasting marital assets (except in the usual course of business or for the necessities of life), harassing the other person, removing the child from the state without the consent of the other party, and from removing the other party or the children from insurance. The injunction is printed on both the Petition and Summons, so both parties are considered to have been put on notice. Failure to comply with the injunction could result in a contempt charge and conviction against you, for which you could face jail, a fine, or both.

Here is the exact language of the injunction, for your convenience:

§ 14-10-107 (b) (I) Upon the filing of a petition for dissolution of marriage or legal separation by the petitioner or co-petitioner or by a legal guardian or conservator on behalf of one of the parties and upon personal service of the petition and summons on the respondent or upon waiver and acceptance of service by the respondent, a temporary injunction shall be in effect against both parties until the final decree is entered or the petition is dismissed or until further order of the court:

(A) Restraining both parties from transferring, encumbering, concealing, or in any way disposing of, without the consent of the other party or an order of the court, any marital property, except in the usual course of business or for the necessities of life and requiring each party to notify the other party of any proposed extraordinary expenditures and to account to the court for all extraordinary expenditures made after the injunction is in effect;

(B) Enjoining both parties from molesting or disturbing the peace of the other party;

(C) Restraining both parties from removing the minor child or children of the parties, if any, from the state without the consent of the other party or an order of the court; and

(D) Restraining both parties, without at least fourteen days' advance notification and the written consent of the other party or an order of the court, from canceling, modifying, terminating, or allowing to lapse for nonpayment of premiums, any policy of health insurance, homeowner's or renter's insurance, or automobile insurance that provides coverage to either of the parties or the minor children or any policy of life insurance that names either of the parties or the minor children as a beneficiary.

Remember: If you do not obey the injunction, you could be held in contempt.

THE CASE MANAGEMENT ORDER

Typically, after you file a petition or motion, the court will mail out the case management order (or may hand it to you while you're there filing your petition or motion). The case management order spells out the requirements for how your case will move forward.

The case management order can seem like an overwhelming document because it is long and often people automatically assume that they aren't going to understand legal documents. Read this document. It tells you exactly what you need to do and the deadlines for your case that are specific to that court. This document tells you everything you need to know and the judge expects you to follow it. It's just like a roadmap.

I recommend you go through the document and highlight every deadline in it. Then, calendar each deadline with one-week advance reminders and, as you do, check them off to ensure you calendared all the deadlines. You might also want to highlight anything you do not understand and take it to a legal aid clinic to ask about those parts to ensure you do everything you are required to do.

If you do not get a case management order, you may want to call the judge's clerk and ask if you should be expecting one. You can find the clerk's number on the Colorado Court website by searching for your district, then by judge, and then calling the number by the judge's name.

Failure to follow the deadlines and requirements in the case management order can result in contempt, denial of evidence, or even dismissal of your case.

THE INITIAL STATUS CONFERENCE

The Initial Status Conference (ISC) is typically an in-person meeting (although sometimes these can be by phone) at the courthouse between the judge or the Family Court Facilitator and the parties. This is a scheduling conference which is supposed to take place within 42 days of filing your petition or motion, where the court will give you deadlines to make sure the case moves forward.

The deadlines you will set are 1) exchange of financial disclosures and 2) when to attend mediation if there are any disputed issues. Some courts will also let you schedule a temporary orders hearing and/or a permanent orders hearing at that time. You must complete mediation before trial for temporary or permanent orders. The reason is because the court hopes you will settle, and it wants to keep court dates available for those who are definitely going to trial.

TIP: The ISC is not a trial. You do not need to prepare evidence in advance. You should bring your calendar with you so you can calendar deadlines and clear dates.

At the ISC, you will let the court know if you think you'll need any experts in your case, such as appraisers, business valuation experts, and child and family investigators, among others. Turn to Chapter 7 to help you determine the types of experts you may need and where to find them.

The next court appearance will typically be either a temporary orders hearing or a permanent orders hearing. A temporary orders hearing is where you can ask the court to issue orders for things like support to be paid or bills to be paid during the pendency of the divorce. A permanent orders hearing is your final hearing in the case (the final divorce hearing). If you filed a motion rather than a petition, the court will not let you set a temporary orders hearing and will just schedule a final motions hearing.

Sometimes the ISC judges will issue interim orders, which order a party to do something between that date and the temporary orders hearing, such as paying support.

Not all courts set an ISC after the filing of a motion because they are only required after filing a new case. Some only conduct ISCs for petitions filed. Alternatively, the courts that do not schedule these may instead set a telephone status conference to relay deadlines and next steps to the parties or require the parties to rely on the Case Management Order.

The rule mandating initial status conferences can be found at C.R.C.P. 16.2(c).

TIP: Some District Courts in Colorado offer Legal Aid Clinics, where you can go in a certain day of the week and talk to lawyer for free. If you don't know what to file, or you want help along the way, check out one of these clinics! Visit the Court website and look under your county or district. You can also call the courthouse and ask what legal aid services are available.

LITIGATION

Litigation refers to the process of carrying on your case, between the filing of the case and resolution. It's "the middle." In a domestic relations case, this process usually involves engaging in disclosures, potentially discovery, possibly a temporary orders hearing, filing of motions (usually if someone is allegedly not doing something they are supposed to be doing), and investigation.

FINANCIAL DISCLOSURES, WITNESS DISCLOSURES, AND DISCOVERY

After you file the petition or motion if the case concerns financial issues like child support, you have 42 days to exchange financial disclosures. After your initial status conference, you may also decide you want to request more information than you got in disclosures, through the process of discovery.

Details on disclosures and discovery are in Chapter 6.

PARENTING CLASS

If you are going through a divorce or initial custody case, you will be required to take a parenting class. This is mandated by law to teach parents how to effectively co-parent with each other despite the animosity of the break-up. It is typically a four-hour class that takes place on one Saturday, but online classes are available to parents who live out of the state or travel often. You are required to complete this class before the final hearing in your case, but read your case management order, because some judges require parents to complete the class 60 days into the pendency of the case.

The statute requiring you to take a parenting class can be found at § 14-10-123.7, C.R.S.

OPPOSING COUNSEL

Lawyer jokes are often based on the premise that lawyers are unpleasant people and are probably written by opposing parties much of the time. For example:

> *What's the difference between a good lawyer and a bad lawyer? A bad lawyer might let a case drag on for several years. A good lawyer knows how to make it last even longer.*
>
> *What's the difference between a lawyer and a jellyfish? One is a spineless, poisonous blob. The other is a form of sea life.*
>
> ... [sigh]

Becoming a lawyer does not make a good person bad. That said, there is a chance you will not like the opposing lawyer. This is not because lawyers are bad people. It is because the opposing lawyer is advocating for your ex on positions which are diametrically opposed to yours.

Most family lawyers are really wonderful people and will treat you with respect and kindness even though they disagree with you. I hope you have one of those on the other side.

I have also worked with rude opposing counsel who, despite not knowing anything about my client, insulted them as a parent and spouse. These lawyers may accuse you of lying, being selfish, and having bad priorities concerning your children. It will make you wonder if family lawyers feed on the bottled tears of their opponents. These types of attorneys think they have to be nasty to show their clients they are fighting for them. We call this "grandstanding."

These lawyers are jerks, and although they are few and far between, that won't matter if you have one on the other side. It will be hard not to take their insults personally. Having been in the game for over ten years, I can attest to this 100%. My advice to you is this: Don't engage in the nastiness. Remind yourself that they are disagreeing with you because they are being paid to and they are being rude because they are jerks. It is not a reflection of you. There is never an excuse to treat anyone like that. You are better than that.

Remember the words of Teddy Roosevelt: "Talk softly and carry a big stick." Be professional and put your energy into building your case rather than sparring with the other side. Wait until you have the assistance of a mediator to engage in settlement negotiations. If you are dealing with a particularly abusive attorney, only communicate with them in email. Keep your communications congenial even if you are not getting the same courtesy back, because remember the rule of communications: Don't put anything in writing you don't want the judge to see.

TEMPORARY ORDERS HEARING

A temporary orders hearing is a hearing or trial that addresses matters that cannot wait until the permanent orders hearing. These are only allowed in pre-decree cases. The disputes you may need addressed quickly are those concerning parenting time, payment of debts, family support, use of the marital home, and other matters the parties are unable to resolve between themselves, that needs to be resolved prior to final resolution in the case. You must request the temporary orders hearing typically at the Initial Status Conference, but if you realize after the ISC that you need one, you can file a motion asking for one. Depending on the docket, it may make more sense to just set the Permanent Orders Hearing. What I mean by this is if the court can set your Permanent Orders Hearing on the same day it could set your Temporary Orders Hearing, and you believe you have enough information to finish the case, then just set the Permanent Orders Hearing. The only reason to set a Temporary Orders Hearing is if you have the type of case that will go on a long time because there is a need for a great deal of discovery to take place, so you are not yet ready for the Permanent Orders Hearing but you have a need for support while the case is pending. If you have a simple divorce, just set the final hearing and be done.

MOTIONS

The word “motion” is synonymous with “request.” A motion to modify parenting time is a request to modify parenting time. There are many reasons you might need to file motions. You may need to file one to modify existing orders. You may need to file one in the middle of a case to ask the court to compel the other side to comply with disclosure or discovery requirements. You may need to file an emergency motion to restrict parenting time or compel compliance with the mandatory injunction not to waste marital assets in the middle of a case. Maybe you need to file a motion to waive the mediation requirement if there is a history of domestic violence or the other side just refuses to cooperate in scheduling.

During the pendency of the case, whether it began by Petition or Motion, parties may file motions asking the court to address things such as non-disclosure, refusal to answer discovery, violations of the injunction, and other matters that come up that cannot wait until the end of the case. The court may resolve the motions by issuing a written ruling or holding a hearing. Depending on the relief requested in the motion, the court may choose to hear the contempt motion in a separate hearing or with the final motions hearing or permanent orders hearing. This is common when contempt motions are filed.

C.R.C.P. 121, § 1-15 governs filing motions in Colorado. This rule says there is a motion, a response, and a reply. That means if you file a motion, the other side gets to file a response, and you get to file a reply. You cannot bring up new information in the reply – you can only rebut the arguments in the response. The way these should be captioned are: "Motion to *blah blah blah*"; "Response to Motion to *blah blah blah*"; and "Reply in Support of Motion to *blah blah blah*."

C.R.C.P. 121, § 1-15 also requires parties confer before filing any motions. That means you must contact the other party and try to work out the difference between yourselves. I advise you to really try and work disagreements out with your ex rather than running to court every time you two disagree. Otherwise, you will both get a reputation for being difficult and this could hurt you later. I in no way mean to discourage you from filing motions. If you need the assistance of the Court, then by all means file a motion. But try to work things out first to try and minimize the motions practice.

This rule also says motions should be no more than 10 pages long. This means you must be concise in your motion. Judges have short attention spans because they are very busy, so I recommend trying to keep motions to 5 pages or less.

When you file a motion, it is said you are "moving" the court to do something. So, you don't say that you are motioning the court; you say you are *moving* the court.

All motions must be supported in law. This is called "authority." This means, you have to cite the law that says you are allowed to file the motion to ask for what you are asking for. You can find some of the more commonly cited authority in Chapter 4 - <u>How to Find the Law</u>, but you can consult with an attorney in a legal aid clinic to ask for assistance.

In law school, we are taught to present our arguments in "IRAC" format:

- **<u>Issue/Introduction</u>**. E.g.: "Petitioner, David Seville, hereby moves the court to *blah blah blah*, and states as follows." This should include some background for the Court. E.g.: "The parties were married on January 11, 2015. The parties divorced on January 10, 2016. The parties have 3 children: Simon Seville, age 15; Alvin Seville, age 13; and Theodore Seville, age 12.
- **<u>Rule</u>** of Law. Cite the law that governs what you are requesting. This is your authority. If you are unsure, consult with an attorney in a legal aid clinic.
- **<u>Application</u>** of Law to Facts. This is where you ask for what you want, explain why you should get it, and tie that into the law you cited. Why should you win, based on what the law says?
- **<u>Conclusion</u>**. 2-3 sentences summarizing what your motion is.

This format makes it easy for the Court to follow along and ensures you include the necessary elements of your argument in your motion.

TIP: Don't use rhetoric or personally attack the other side/ counsel.

There is a difference between explaining to the court why the other side's argument is weak, and personally insulting them. Stay away from allegations that they are lying or being misleading. The Court does not want to hear this. Instead, you can say that the other side's recitation of facts is "inaccurate" and explain why.

In conclusion, be professional and concise. Get to the point of why you are seeking the relief you are seeking.

MEDIATION

Mediation is a meeting between you and the other party where you engage in negotiations with the help of a neutral third party, called a mediator, who helps you try and reach a resolution with the other party. Most courts require all parties to engage in at least one mediation prior to coming to court for any hearing.

Movies portray mediation as a witty exchange of offers and random recitations of law between attorneys, interrupted sporadically by the parties throwing cunning insults at each other across a large conference room table. While this may be fun to watch on TV, this would not be pleasant if you were one of the parties.

In real life, you have the option of doing mediation in separate rooms with the mediator going back and forth between the rooms to deliver offers and discuss options. Some mediators believe it is more effective if everyone sits in the same room. You are the one who gets to make this choice, and you can absolutely refuse to be in the same room as the ex during mediation.

There are attorney mediators, former judges who mediate, and non-attorney mediators. Mediator rates tend to range from $120 per hour all the way up to $400 per hour and up. The mediation cost is typically split evenly between the parties, with a two-hour minimum requirement (as this is what the court will require you to do).

So how do you choose a mediator? The Court website has a list of approved mediators who conduct mediation through the court's Office of Dispute Resolution. A link is provided in the Appendix of this book. Most attorneys tend to use the same people over and over again because they discover who they like, who is good at getting cases resolved, and who is merely a mouthpiece. Consulting with an attorney at a free legal aid clinic may be a good place to go to ask for referrals.

THE FINAL HEARING

If your case does not resolve in settlement, then your case will resolve either with a permanent orders hearing or a final motions hearing. Section 3 of this book covers how to prepare and present your case for trial in greater detail. Here is a brief overview of what the final hearing looks like.

A permanent orders hearing refers to the final hearing in a pre-decree case, which will resolve all outstanding disputes. Permanent orders replace any temporary orders that were in place before. A final motions hearing refers to a final hearing in a post-decree case, which will resolve the outstanding motions pending.

Usually the person who initiated the action presents their case first. This means they call their witnesses first. If you are there on a divorce or initial custody case, the Petitioner will go first. If you are there on a motion to modify, enforce, or a contempt motion, the person who filed the motion (the movant) goes first. If you both filed motions, it may be the person who filed the first motion, or it may be the Petitioner.

Each side can make an opening statement. This tells the judge what each party is asking for and what evidence the judge will hear that will support the request.

Whichever party goes first will call their own witnesses first. Questioning your own witnesses is called direct examination. After each witness is done with direct examination, the other side gets to question them before they leave the witness stand. Questioning the other side's witnesses is called cross examination. After cross examination, the other party gets to do redirect, to rebut anything that came out during cross examination. You cannot ask questions on redirect that were not a part of the cross examination.

It is through witnesses (including yourself) that you will enter evidence such as text messages, emails, medical records, and the like, which you intend to use to support your case. After the first side rests her case, it is the other side's turn to call his witnesses. Usually he will call himself as the first witness. He may then call other people as witnesses. Once you rest, the other side may want to call rebuttal witnesses to rebut bad facts that came out when you put on your case. Depending on how much time is left in the day, the judge may or may not allow this.

To answer the question burning on your mind right this second: No, you will not ask yourself questions and then answer them. That would be silly, and I'd like to see someone do that some time, but don't let it be you. You will just talk to testify on your own behalf.

Judges typically time each side by when they are questioning witnesses (on direct or cross), and they allow each side an equal amount of time to put on their respective cases. So as an example, you may each have three hours to put on your case, which includes questioning witnesses, opening statement, and closing argument. Use it wisely.

Last, you'll make closing arguments. Then the judge will either issue a ruling right then or "take the case on advisement" meaning she will review her notes and issue a ruling at a later date.

CHAPTER 2: JURISDICTION AND VENUE

Jurisdiction refers to the Court's authority to preside over and rule on a case. If a court has no jurisdiction, it cannot accept the filing of your case, and as a result cannot issue orders in that case. An obvious example would be if you and your ex have no affiliation with Colorado (never lived there, never been there), Colorado would have no jurisdiction to accept your divorce case.

First, you must determine whether the Court has jurisdiction by ensuring you have met the requirements in this chapter to file the case. Then, you must ensure the Court has jurisdiction over the other party by ensuring you have the other party served properly. In order for the Court to have personal jurisdiction over you in a domestic relations case, you must either be the one who filed the case, must have waived service, or must have been served by personal service in accordance with C.R.C.P. Rule 4. The Court can assert personal jurisdiction over the other party even if they reside in a different state. You must still have that person served but can hire a process server in the state where they reside and have them served there. Service of process must comply with the requirements of C.R.C.P. Rule 4.

Once you determine Colorado has jurisdiction to accept your case, you then have to decide which court to file in. **Venue** refers to which district or county court is proper for your case in the State which has jurisdiction. Domestic relations cases can be filed in any county where either party lives. If you are unsure which county you should file in, you can consult with an attorney in a legal aid clinic. Depending on the circumstances of your case, you may find it more or less favorable to file in one county versus the other.

Before filing your divorce or legal separation, you or the other spouse must have been a resident of Colorado for at least 91 days immediately prior to commencing the case. **§ 14-10-106, C.R.S.**

Child custody jurisdiction is governed by the Uniform Child Custody Jurisdiction Enforcement Act (UCCJEA), which can be found at § 14-13-101, et seq. The UCCJEA has been adopted by 49 out of the 50 states (Massachusetts being the sole hold-out) so that the states would have uniform laws on jurisdiction and enforcement of custody orders. This happened because before the UCCJEA, parents used to abscond with their own children and move to other states and try to get more favorable orders, resulting in conflicting orders and states fighting over jurisdiction and enforcement. States that adopted the UCCJEA have agreed to enforce the other states' orders on custody and not enter conflicting orders.

> **Before filing your Petition for custody (Allocation of Parental Responsibilities)** case, one parent must be present in the state, and there can be no other orders concerning this child in another state. Colorado must be the child's "home state" meaning the child has lived here for at least 182 days, OR the child did live here for at least 182 days, and no more than 182 has passed since the child has been absent from the state and a parent still lives here, OR if the child is less than six months of age, the child must have resided here since birth **§ 14-13-201, C.R.S.**
>
> If you are seeking to **modify another State's cus-**

tody order here in Colorado, you must request a transfer of jurisdiction from the other state to Colorado first. In order to do that, one parent must be present in the state, and Colorado must be the child's "home state" meaning the child has lived here for at least 182 days. **§ 14-13-201, C.R.S.** If you are seeking to **modify custody on an emergency basis**, you may file a motion to restrict at any time, asking the court to assume temporary emergency jurisdiction under § 14-13-204, C.R.S.

If you are filing a new child support case, you can do this two ways. You can either file a custody case in Colorado and the Court will enter a child support order as part of the custody determination, or you can contact the Child Support Enforcement Unit ("CSE") to help you establish child support (without establishing a custody order). If the other party lives in another State, you can still file the case here as long as you meet the jurisdiction requirements above for filing for custody. However, if you go through CSE, CSE will work with the CSE office in the state where the other party lives, and your order may be issued out of that state if the other party is determined to be the Obligor (the person who owes you child support). If you are seeking to **modify an order that was issued in Colorado**, you may file a motion to modify in Colorado.

If you are seeking to **modify another State's child support order in Colorado,** the obligor must reside in Colorado prior to filing to transfer jurisdiction of the child support case.

Generally, for **Adoptions**, the state where the child lives has jurisdiction to grant the adoption. However, this can be complicated if there are orders or any pending actions concerning the same child in another state. **§ 19-5-201, C.R.S. states "Any child legally available for adoption as provided in section 19-5-203, under eighteen years of age, and either present in the state at the time the petition for adoption is filed or under the jurisdiction of a court in Colorado for at least six months may be adopted." Based on this, if the child has been present in Colorado for six months, but the custody orders were granted in Tennessee where the other parent still resides, either Court may assume jurisdiction over the child for the purposes of an adoption. You could file in Colorado, but you may be in for a jurisdictional fight, in which case the judges in the two states would talk and decide which state is the more convenient forum to decide the issue.**

In **protection order** cases, venue is proper where the parties either reside, or where the alleged incidents occurred that give rise to the need for the protection order. If the incidents occurred in several counties, you should file in the county where the opposing party resides.

SECTION 2 – BUILDING YOUR CASE

When people ask me what the toughest thing was about Army Basic Training, my answer always surprises them. The hardest thing about Boot Camp is staying awake. In addition to drill sergeants yelling in your face, learning to run faster than you've ever run before, road marches for miles and miles in combat boots, learning map reading (especially if you're directionally challenged like me), and shooting a rifle – oh and let's not forget the gas chamber - (yes they actually tear gas us). The hardest part truly is staying awake, because in addition to all that they sleep deprive you. They keep you up until midnight making you clean your rifle for the fifth time that day, and then wake you up at 6:00 AM by throwing a trashcan across the room or using the trashcan and a broom stick the same way a farmer uses a triangle to call the family for dinner. Boot Camp is all about taking people from all walks of life, breaking them down, and then building them up into one type of person – a soldier.

Becoming a soldier tests your endurance for things you never thought you could overcome. Soldiers graduate Boot Camp confident and brave, and willing to do anything including die for their country because they've proven to themselves there's nothing they can't do. Through every challenge in Boot Camp emerges a strength which becomes the foundation of the budding soldier, which will stay with that soldier forever.

Going through this case will test your endurance and reveal a strength within you that you may not have known was there. Learning the law is like learning a new language. While most people are intimidated by legal documents, you will become a pro at reading and drafting them. As you learn the ins and outs of the legal process, you will gain more and more confidence in your ability to analyze the law, ask tough questions and prepare your case.

And you will do it all probably sleep deprived.

At least no one is teargassing you!

CHAPTER 3: CASE DEADLINES

After you've filed your case, the absolute first thing you need to know is what are your case deadlines? You must calendar your deadlines before building your case to ensure you are in compliance with the court requirements, and you are building your case in a timely manner.

The Colorado Rules of Civil Procedure (C.R.C.P.) govern case deadlines. When a domestic case is started in Colorado, most of our judges mail out a Case Management Order, which lays out all the deadlines for you so you don't have to look them up.

When a motion is filed, or a Petition is served, the clock begins to automatically run on deadlines for your case, so you need to ensure to calendar these dates. Then, when you set the case for trial, the clock begins to run on even more deadlines! So, you will want to go back and calendar those!

TIP: If the Case Management Order conflicts with the C.R.C.P. Rules, follow the Case Management Order.

Here is a snapshot of deadlines you need to calendar at the start of your case:

Count From the date the Petition OR Motion was filed:

- Initial Status Conference must occur within 42 days. This is the responsibility of the Court to set. C.R.C.P. 16.2(C)(1)(E)

Count From the date service of process was completed:

- Response is due within 21 days. C.R.C.P. 12(a).
- Mandatory disclosures and certificate of compliance are due within 42 days. C.R.C.P. 16.2(e)(2).
- The Court may grant your divorce or legal separation 91 days or more after the other party was served with the Petition for Dissolution. **§14-10-106(1)(a)(III).**

Count Backwards from Date Trial is Scheduled:

- 63 days before trial, you must file your list of lay and expert witness disclosures. C.R.C.P. 16.2(e)(3).
- Discovery must have been served on the other party no later than 63 days before trial. C.R.C.P. 16.2
- Expert report is due 56 days before trial. C.R.C.P. 16.2(g)(5).
- All discovery must be completed 28 days before trial (meaning depositions have been taken and discovery responses have been received by this deadline). C.R.C.P. 16.2(f)(5).
- Rebuttal expert reports are due 21 days before trial.
- Trial management certificates are due to the court 7 days before trial. (Note some courts require these 14 days in advance.). C.R.C.P. 16.2(h).
- Exhibits, including an updated Sworn Financial Statement, must be exchanged with the other party 7 days before trial. C.R.C.P. 16.2(h).

CHAPTER 4: HOW TO FIND THE LAW

For the purposes of family law, generally, the law in the United States consists of **statutes** (State laws) and **case law** (also known as common law). Statutes are the laws passed by the Legislature that started out as bills. This is what people generally think of when they refer to "the law" – a book of laws you refer to for an answer to the question, "what's the law on [subject]?"

Because statutes are written by human beings, and human beings are imperfect, sometimes statutes can be open to interpretation. This is why lawyers have jobs. That's where case law comes in. Case law refers to published cases that have already interpreted a certain issue. The cases are published so that in the future, people can see how the higher courts have interpreted certain statutes. That interpretation used by the higher court essentially becomes "law" until either an even higher court interprets the same statute differently, or the Legislature amends the law to clarify it.

When you look up the laws that apply to your case, you should start with the "annotated statutes," which are books that have the statutes and case law interpreting those in one place. Some states list their annotated statutes on certain websites. You can find these in a law library by asking a law librarian for some guidance finding law on your issue. You can also meet with a lawyer for even just one hour to get some help. You can also turn to the internet. Free internet research tools are listed in the Appendix.

You should also call your court and ask if they offer any *pro se* or legal aid clinics. A *pro se* clinic is a service in which lawyers in the local bar volunteer their time to provide legal assistance to self-represented parties, and they typically provide this resource in some empty room at the courthouse.

If you want to contact a lawyer to just provide guidance to help you represent yourself, find law, or be available to provide legal advice, look for lawyers who offer "unbundled services." This is a term that means the lawyer is willing to offer legal services on an **à la carte** basis rather than making you choose between retaining the lawyer for a huge retainer to represent you, or nothing at all. It may help you to simply find out what statutes to look up yourself. Once you find the relevant statute, you'll be able to find the cases interpreting that statute.

You may want to ask the lawyer to draft a "trial brief" for you on the law that applies to your case. A trial brief is a summary of the laws that apply to your case and may even contain argument on how it applies to the facts of your case in support of your position. You may have to pay for a few hours of that lawyer's work depending on how complicated your case is, but this may save you a lot of time. If you cannot afford to pay for hours of a lawyer's time, do not worry. You will just have to do a little more leg work yourself conducting your own research. That's where your local law librarian comes in handy.

A BRIEF SUMMARY OF LAWS YOU MAY NEED TO KNOW

Here are some helpful hints on laws that govern what you may be wanting to do. You should read these before citing them to make sure that this is the proper law you need to cite. Laws provide you guidance on what evidence you need to present in order to prevail.

---

§ 13-14-104.5, 105

Civil Protection Orders

---

§ 14-10-106, C.R.S.

Statute governing court's jurisdiction to grand divorce or legal separation.

---

§ 14-10-107, C.R.S.

Statute containing the mandatory injunction.

---

§ 14-10-108, C.R.S.

Authority to request Temporary Orders, including an order for compliance with mandatory injunction.

---

§ 14-10-112, C.R.S.

Separation Agreements in Divorces and Legal Separations.

---

§ 14-10-113, C.R.S.

Statute governing how the Court divides property. Pay special attention to section (6), which says if you do not submit your written agreement to the PERA administrator within 90 days after entry of your decree, then you lose out on dividing the PERA.

---

§ 14-10-114, C.R.S.

Authority to request temporary and permanent maintenance (spousal support).

§ 14-10-115, C.R.S.

Child Support Statute. This law is the governing authority on initial child support determinations as well as modifications of existing orders. This statute covers calculations, findings of underemployment, deviations from child support calculations, expenses that the court may consider in determining child support, and what is defined as income. This is a must-read in any child support case.

§ 14-10-116.5, C.R.S.

Authority to request appointment of CFI.

§ 14-10-122, C.R.S.

Authority to modify child support and maintenance. If you are seeking to modify your existing support order, read this to determine if you are eligible to modify before filing your motion.

§ 14-10-123, C.R.S.

Authority to commence a custody action, (called Allocation of Parental Rights and Responsibilities) by either a parent or a non-parent who has had the child in their care for at least 182 days.

§ 14-10-123.3, C.R.S.

Motion for grandparent visitation.

§ 14-10-124, C.R.S.

"Best Interest of the Child" statute. This is THE law that lays out what the Judge will be evaluating in a custody determination. This law lists 9 factors the court will be evaluating. You should keep this one handy and make sure that you address all nine factors when presenting your case.

---

§ 14-10-127, C.R.S.

Authority to request appointment of PRE.

---

§ 14-10-129, C.R.S.

Authority to modify parenting time and request relocation with children. If you are seeking to modify your existing parenting time order, read this to determine if you are eligible to modify before filing your motion.

---

§ 14-10-129(4), C.R.S.

Authority for motion to restrict parenting time. This is a subset of the modification statute (directly above) and provides the basis under which you may ask the court to completely restrict the other parent's parenting time.

---

§ 14-10-131, C.R.S.

Authority to modify decision making responsibility. If you are seeking to modify your existing parenting time order, read this to determine if you are eligible to modify before filing your motion.

---

§ 14-13-201, C.R.S.

Statute governing jurisdiction to enter initial child custody determination.

---

§ 14-13-204, C.R.S.

Authority to request court assume temporary emergency jurisdiction.

§ 19-5-201, C.R.S.

Who may be adopted. Child must be available under § 19-5-203, under 18, and must have lived in Colorado for at least six months.

§ 19-5-203, C.R.S.

Availability for adoption. Child may be adopted if the other parent has abandoned the child for more than a year or failed to support the child for more than a year.

C.R.C.P. 4 and 5

Rules governing service of process.

C.R.C.P. 16.2

State court rules governing domestic relations case procedure.

C.R.C.P. 16.2(e)(10)

Authority to request court reopen divorce property division because of fraud.

C.R.C.P. 26

State court rule governing discovery. This rule governs unless otherwise covered or contradicted by C.R.C.P. 16.2(f).

C.R.C.P. 37

Authority to file motion to compel disclosures or discovery responses with request for attorney fees.

C.R.C.P. 107

Contempt.

C.R.C.P. 121, § 1-11

Rulegoverningrequestingacontinuance(reschedulingofahearing).

C.R.C.P. 121, § 1-15

Miscellaneous

Local Court Rules governing filing of motions.

Title 14 governs divorce, custody, child support, and jurisdiction for your case involving your child. When you see a law cited as § 14-10-124, C.R.S., the "14" is the title, the "10" is the article, and the "124" is the section. So, when I refer to Title 14, it's the first number.

Title 19 governs juvenile court matters, including adoption and dependency and neglect.

Title 15 governs probate.

Title 18 governs the criminal code.

PROPERTY AND DEBT DIVISION

In Colorado, the law directs the Court to divide assets and debts "equitably" which means fairly. Note, this does not say "equally." The Court has discretion to award a more or less favorable offset of the assets and debts to one party. Typically, courts try and divide assets and debts equally anyway. It is up to you to explain to the

Court what division you believe is fair and/or equal and the reason why.

Courts decide cases based on evidence and law. Evidence is presented to the court in the form of testimony and tangible things such as documents or pictures. The Court applies the evidence presented to what the law requires the Court consider and determines the outcome of the case.

Because the Court decides cases based on evidence, you cannot go into court and simply say, "I want you to divide assets 50/50" because the judge will have no clue what you're talking about. You need to tell the judge what the assets are and what you believe those values to be and show the judge what evidence you have to back that up. For example, if you want the court to divide bank accounts 50/50, you need to show the court what bank accounts there are, and what the values of each account is.

Back in the olden days, spouses had to have a valid legal basis to obtain a divorce, such as abandonment, infidelity, or some other "marital misconduct." Without a valid legal basis, spouses who wished to divorce were out of luck. Those days are gone, and now you do not need a reason to get divorced. As a result, Colorado is considered a "no-fault state." The only reason you must assert to get divorced is that your marriage is irretrievably broken. The other party does not have to agree with this, and you can get divorced even if the other spouse does not want to, and even if they refuse to participate in the divorce.

Because Colorado is a no-fault state, you cannot ask the Court to consider fault in its custody determination, unless you can show it is related to the best interests of the children. Likewise, you cannot ask the Court to consider fault in dividing financial assets and debts unless you can show that the fault somehow unfairly depleted what you would be entitled to, and that it was done in contemplation of divorce. The Court won't let you go back through years of irresponsible spending by your ex in order to get more money. Courts typically are willing to look back into the marriage about six months for financial misbehavior in considering an equitable division.

Some examples are as follows:

> It is irrelevant that your spouse is promiscuous and had multiple affairs, UNLESS you can show that the spouse was having those sexual encounters while the children were present in the home and maybe even aware of what was happening.
>
> It is irrelevant that your spouse is an irresponsible spendthrift, UNLESS you can show that your spouse blew $20,000 in Blackhawk and bought a Harley Davidson right before filing for divorce, just to screw you out of marital funds and stick you with half the debt.

There is no guarantee the judge will let you present your fault-based argument, even if you believe you have a good reason. These are largely emotional, which carry no weight. If the judge shuts you down before you can get it out, ask the judge to "make a record." This essentially means you believe the judge is making an error, and you want to preserve your position for appeal. When you ask to make a record, the judge will let you talk. Then you can explain why you believe the evidence you want to present is relevant to the issue the judge must decide, and you can ask the judge to reconsider. If you are still shot down, then let it go. You successfully preserved it for appeal, and that is the next route you would have to take.

Attorneys typically use Asset Division Spreadsheets to present a snapshot of assets and debts to the Court. These spreadsheets summarize the assets within certain categories, the value of each, and show the court the value that each party will walk away with if the court divides the assets the way they are asking. Here is a sample:

Asset:	FMV:	Loan:	Net Equity:	Non-Marital:	Net Marital:	Husband:	Wife:
TANGIBLE PROPERTY							
House	$ 500,000.00	$ 360,000.00	$ 140,000.00		$ 140,000.00	$ 29,250.00	$ 110,750.00
Wife Car	$ 25,000.00	$ 20,000.00	$ 5,000.00		$ 5,000.00		$ 5,000.00
Husband Car	$ 16,000.00	$ 20,000.00	$ (4,000.00)		$ (4,000.00)	$ (4,000.00)	
Total	**$ 541,000.00**	**$ 400,000.00**	**$ 141,000.00**	**$ -**	**$ 141,000.00**	**$ 25,250.00**	**$ 115,750.00**
BANK ACCOUNTS/CASH							
Wells Fargo Checking	$ 1,500.00		$ 1,500.00		$ 1,500.00		$ 1,500.00
Wells Fargo Savings	$ 10,000.00		$ 10,000.00		$ 10,000.00	$ 5,000.00	$ 5,000.00
Total	**$ 11,500.00**	**$ -**	**$ 11,500.00**	**$ -**	**$ 11,500.00**	**$ 5,000.00**	**$ 6,500.00**
RETIREMENT							
Husband 401k	$ 100,000.00		$ 100,000.00		$ 100,000.00	$ 85,000.00	$ 15,000.00
Wife IRA	$ 120,000.00		$ 120,000.00	$ 50,000.00	$ 70,000.00		$ 70,000.00
Total	**$ 220,000.00**	**$ -**	**$ 220,000.00**	**$ 50,000.00**	**$ 170,000.00**	**$ 85,000.00**	**$ 85,000.00**
MISC.							
Business	$ 100,000.00		$ 100,000.00		$ 100,000.00	$ 100,000.00	
Total	**$ 100,000.00**	**$ -**	**$ 100,000.00**	**$ -**	**$ 100,000.00**	**$ 100,000.00**	**$ -**
DEBTS							
Capital One	$ (8,000.00)		$ (8,000.00)		$ (8,000.00)	$ (8,000.00)	
Total	**$ (8,000.00)**	**$ -**	**$ (8,000.00)**	**$ -**	**$ (8,000.00)**	**$ (8,000.00)**	**$ -**
Totals:	**$ 864,500.00**	**$ 400,000.00**	**$ 464,500.00**	**$ 50,000.00**	**$ 414,500.00**	**$ 207,250.00**	**$ 207,250.00**
Equalization Payment:						$ -	$ -
Grand Totals:						$ 207,250.00	$ 207,250.00

The sample categorizes the assets and debts by tangible property, cash accounts, retirement assets, miscellaneous and debts. The next column, "FMV" is the fair market value of the asset. This is where you would list the value of your home. The next column,

Loan, is where you would put the loan on the home. The third column subtracts Loan from FMV for a Net Equity value of that home. As you can see, these columns usually only pertain to homes and cars, which is why the Net Equity and FMV columns are the same for all other listed items.

The Non-Marital column is where you will put the value of your non-marital portion of the asset. In this example, Wife listed $50,000 of non-marital value to her IRA. This could be because at the time she married, her IRA was worth $50,000. Now it is worth $220,000. By listing $50,000 of non-marital value, she is letting the court know that this needs to be subtracted from what the Court is dividing in the divorce. The next column, Net Marital, is the column showing all the marital property to be divided in this divorce. The last two columns are used to apportion the marital property between Husband and Wife. The bottom rows are used to add up the assets and debts to ensure that what is being apportioned to Husband and Wife end up in an equal division.

If you use an Asset Division Spreadsheet, make sure you also bring supporting documentation to Court for every value you entered. Courts appreciate you summarizing your position concisely like this, but only if it is based on accurate information.

The example here shows an equal division of assets. The bottom line is affected by how the parties may value the assets listed. You may value the gun collection at $10,000 and your ex may value it at $100. For things like collectibles, you may need an expert to come up with a professional valuation to use. Bank accounts are easier to value because the amount in the account is stated clearly on the account statement or web page. While it is true that bank account values change daily (as do stocks and other account values), you may put the value as of a specific date on the asset division spreadsheet. Just be sure that the spreadsheet gives the court an accurate estimate of what is to be divided.

You will note I put the Retirement Assets in a different color on the Asset Division Spreadsheet. This is because these may have a different tax consequence than the other assets listed, which needs to be accounted for. If you have retirement assets that consist of pre-tax money, you either need to adjust the value to account for taxes (if dividing amongst the other assets) or divide these separately with other similar assets.

The IRS says that exchanges of property for the purpose of divorce is a non-taxable event. That means if you get half the other spouse's 401(k), you get it without paying the penalty you'd otherwise pay for withdrawing funds from a 401(k) prematurely. You do not get it in cash though. You get it in the form of a tax-deferred asset, such as a traditional IRA.

If you are a business owner, you may be wondering if you are going to have to give your ex half the business. The answer is no. If you two own the business together, then the answer is, of course, yes. But if it is your own business, then the Court is not going to issue an order making your ex a partner- the Court does not have jurisdiction to do that.

The way this is "divided up" is that the business will be valued, and that value will be placed in your column on the asset division spreadsheet to account for the value of that asset that you are getting. This will result in your ex getting a more favorable offset of the remaining assets and debts.

What you need to do is have the business valued and ask the court to allocate assets to the ex that are worth half of the value of that business. The ex will be entitled to receive all of the business financials, such as bank statements, balance sheets and income statements, so the ex can also obtain their own valuation if they so choose. Many business owners have a problem with this. However, if you hold anything back, the Court can sanction you for failing to properly disclose. What you can do to protect yourself though is insist that the ex sign a confidentiality agreement that they will not disclose the financials you disclose to them. If they refuse, you may refuse to provide the financials and ask the Court to order a confidentiality mandate. If the ex then breaks it, you can ask the court to hold them in contempt.

Review § 14-10-113, C.R.S. to ensure you address all the factors the Court may consider in deciding your assets and debts.

CHILD SUPPORT AND MAINTENANCE

Family Support consists of two types of payments: maintenance (also known as spousal support or alimony) and child support. Maintenance is support paid by the higher income earning spouse to the lower income earner and has nothing to do with children. Child support is ordered when there are children. In many cases, courts order both maintenance and child support to be paid. Both of these are calculated using statutory calculations crafted by our Legislature.

To access the child support and maintenance online calculator, you can either Google "Colorado Courts Child Support" and click on the first link, or you can type this URL into your browser: https://www.courts.state.co.us/Forms/Forms_List.cfm?-Form_Type_ID=94

The website will have you download a child support calculator from where you can calculate child support and maintenance.

The Court usually orders the paying parent to pay the exact amount the calculation comes up with for child support. However, the maintenance calculation is typically only a starting point for the Court, from which the Court may deviate up or down based on other information provided by the parties. When both are ordered, the courts are careful to ensure the recipient does not receive a windfall and the payor can still pay their reasonable expenses.

To calculate these you will need to know your ex's income, health insurance amounts for the kids (for child support), and whether you want to ask the court to throw extraordinary children's expenses into the calculation or if you and the ex are just going to work that out yourselves. This information will be provided in disclosures.

When considering incomes of the parties, usually any source of income counts for purposes of calculating child support and maintenance. With child support, the inquiry usually ends there. With maintenance, spouses have more wiggle room to argue for a deviation up or down based on several factors, such as:

(I) The financial resources of the recipient spouse, including the actual or potential income from separate or marital property or any other source and the ability of the recipient spouse to meet his or her needs independently;

(II) The financial resources of the payor spouse, including the actual or potential income from separate or marital property or any other source and the ability of the payor spouse to meet his or her reasonable needs while paying maintenance;

(III) The lifestyle during the marriage;

(IV) The distribution of marital property, including whether additional marital property may be awarded to reduce or alleviate the need for maintenance;

(V) Both parties' income, employment, and employability, obtainable through reasonable diligence and additional training or education, if necessary, and any necessary reduction in employment due to the needs of an unemancipated child of the marriage or the circumstances of the parties;

(VI) Whether one party has historically earned higher or lower income than the income reflected at the time of permanent orders and the duration and consistency of income from overtime or secondary employment;

(VII) The duration of the marriage;

(VIII) The amount of temporary maintenance and the number of months that temporary maintenance was paid to the recipient spouse;

(IX) The age and health of the parties, including consideration of significant health care needs or uninsured or unreimbursed health care expenses;

(X) Significant economic or noneconomic contribution to the marriage or to the economic, educational, or occupational advancement of a party, including but not limited to completing an education or job training, payment by one spouse of the other spouse's separate debts, or enhancement of the other spouse's personal or real property;

(XI) Whether the circumstances of the parties at the time of permanent orders warrant the award of a nominal amount of maintenance in order to preserve a claim of maintenance in the future;

(XII) Whether the maintenance is deductible for federal income tax purposes by the payor and taxable income to the recipient, and any adjustments to the amount of maintenance to equitably allocate the tax burden between the parties.

Often, if you are arguing against paying maintenance, you basically need to show the other spouse does not have a need for it. If you are trying to get maintenance, you will want to show you do have a need for it. The above list will be helpful to you in arguing for or against a maintenance award. The list is taken directly from § 14-10-114, C.R.S. and is not exhaustive but will help you formulate your arguments.

When calculating incomes of the parties in determining maintenance and child support, the Court will use income from pretty much any source, including:

- Income from employment
- Tips
- Commissions
- Overtime pay
- Bonuses
- Dividends
- Severance pay
- Pensions income
- In-kind payments
- Royalties
- Rents
- Interest
- Trust income

- Annuities
- Capital gains
- Workers' compensation benefits
- Social security benefits
- Unemployment payments
- Disability insurance benefits
- Insurance payments
- Monetary gifts
- Lottery winnings
- Investment Income
- Expense reimbursements
- Alimony

TIP: The Court often won't include overtime if it is voluntarily worked and not a requirement of your employment.

Social security payments for your child do not count as income. Income from second jobs usually will not count if this requires you to work more than a 40-hour work week. The general rule is the Court does not want to calculate based on income that requires you to work more than 40 hours. Child support received does not count as income because that is considered income of the child. If you are self-employed, you can deduct your ordinary and necessary expenses from your income.

The Court has the discretion to deviate up or down from both child support and maintenance. However, it is rare for the Court to deviate from the child support calculation than it is for maintenance. When considering whether to deviate from the calculation, the court can consider whether a spouse is intentionally unemployed or underemployed, whether the spouse is in an education program designed to or reasonably intended to result in a degree or certification within a reasonable period of time; completing the program will result in a higher income; the program is a good faith career choice that is not intended to deprive the child of support; and the parent's participation in the program does not unreasonably reduce the amount of child support available to a child. In determining whether a spouse is intentionally underemployed or unemployed, the Court will look at the persons job search, training, and employment opportunities in that field, as well as the person's employment history.

Lastly, the Court will not deviate from child support unless the Court finds the deviation is in the best interests of the child.

A description of how child support is calculated can be found in § 14-10-115, C.R.S. The maintenance calculation formula can be found at § 14-10-114, C.R.S. Modification of these is governed by § 14-10-122, C.R.S.

THE CHILD SUPPORT ENFORCEMENT AGENCY

You can seek child support either through the Court by filing an APR case or through the Child Support Enforcement Agency (CSE). How do you choose whether to file an APR case or go through CSE? That depends on whether you want a custody order with the child support order or not. If you just want the child support established without having a custody order, then CSE may be the better option for you. Here is a pro/con list of going through CSE versus the State Court:

CSE Pro	CSE Con
Typically, no need for lawyers. CSE Caseworker will guide you through the process.	Some people still want lawyers to engage in more in-depth discovery to uncover income or help them contest the child support calculation CSE came up with.
CSE has parties fill out financial questionnaire and comes up with child support calculation.	CSE does not engage in discovery to uncover hidden income.
CSE only handles child support.	You will not get a custody order from CSE.
CSE gives you 15 days to contest the child support calculation and request a hearing.	You need to make sure you are checking your mail daily because if you miss the 15-day deadline you are out of luck.
CSE is free to use.	CSE is a government agency and as a result, the process can drag on for a year.
CSE will track down the other party if you just have a last known address.	No con. This is pretty cool.
CSE can intercept the obligor's tax return and give it to you if they owe you child support.	No con. This is also pretty cool.

CSE is pretty cool because it is a free service and you get child support figured out. The only drawback really is that it can take longer to get your order, but depending on your court's backlog, it may end up being a wash anyway. Also, if you need to file a custody case, you should file a Petition for Allocation of Parental Responsibilities and let the court figure out child support with that case rather than have both a DR case and a CSE matter open. If you are unsure on what to do, consult with an attorney in a legal aid clinic for assistance.

CUSTODY

In Colorado, the courts do not use the term "custody" anymore. Instead, custody is referred to as "Allocation of Parental Rights and Responsibilities" or APR for short. I will refer to both APR and custody to mean the same thing in this book because "custody" is the word most people are familiar with.

APR refers to allocation of parenting time and allocation of decision-making responsibility and is decided based on what is in the best interests of the child. The statutes governing custody list several factors the Court must consider when determining what is in the best interests of the child, but this list is not exclusive, and the Court may consider any factor it deems relevant to the determination.

In determining what is in the best interests of the child, the Court starts with § 14-10-124, C.R.S., which outlines a list of factors the court is to consider:

- The wishes of the child's parents as to parenting time;
- The wishes of the child if he or she is sufficiently mature to express reasoned and independent preferences as to the parenting time schedule;
- The interaction and interrelationship of the child with his or her parents, his or her siblings, and any other person who may significantly affect the child's best interests;
- The child's adjustment to his or her home, school, and community;
- The mental and physical health of all individuals involved, except that a disability alone shall not be a basis to deny or restrict parenting time;
- The ability of the parties to encourage the sharing of love, af-

fection, and contact between the child and the other party; except that, if the court determines that a party is acting to protect the child from witnessing domestic violence or from being a victim of child abuse or neglect or domestic violence, the party's protective actions shall not be considered with respect to this factor;

- Whether the past pattern of involvement of the parties with the child reflects a system of values, time commitment, and mutual support;
- The physical proximity of the parties to each other as this relates to the practical considerations of parenting time;
- The ability of each party to place the needs of the child ahead of his or her own needs.

TIP: Whatever you are asking for in terms of custody, you need to show why it is in the best interests of your child.

Do not go into Court and argue "rights" such as "Father's rights," etc. Father's rights is a marketing term used by law firms. There is no such thing when it comes to custody. Custody is based on what is in the best interests of the child, and that has nothing to do with the perceived "rights" of either parent.

Decision making responsibility refers to decisions concerning the child's education and medical decisions. Courts prefer to award joint decision making, meaning you and the ex will be required to discuss these things and compromise. This is called coparenting. However, the Courts realize sometimes this is impossible depending on the family dynamic, such as a history of domestic violence. Therefore, in addition to the above best interest factors, the Court considers the following factors when determining whether or not to award joint or sole decision making:

- Credible evidence of the ability of the parties to cooperate and to make decisions jointly;
- Whether the past pattern of involvement of the parties with the child reflects a system of values, time commitment, and mutual support that would indicate an ability as mutual decision makers to provide a positive and nourishing relationship with the child;
- Whether an allocation of mutual decision-making responsibility on any one or a number of issues will promote more frequent or continuing contact between the child and each of the parties.

These lists are short excerpts of the APR and decision-making statutes. You should read them fully to get an idea of everything the Court will consider and to fully understand your burden of proof. In addition, there is a lot of case law out there interpreting the APR statutes, and in all likelihood there is case law that you could compare to your own case to help you argue for what you are asking for. A good place to start is by reading the annotated statutes. You can also conduct keyword searches using Google Scholar Legal Research. A full list of free legal research resources is available in the Appendix. You may also want to meet with an attorney in a free legal aid clinic to help guide you in the right direction. Often, attorneys can cite cases that pertain to a particular rule of law off the top of their heads.

Use the law to explain to the Court why your request is in the best interests of your child. If you have bad facts against you, explain to the Court using the law what you plan to do differently and what action steps you'll take to achieve that goal. For example, if you have been involved in domestic violence, take a domestic violence reform or victim class, or anger management. Show the Court you are serious about improving yourself for your child. The Court wants to know you are safe and will put the child's needs ahead of your own. The Court is not looking for perfect parents with perfect pasts.

Review the following statutes to ensure you address all the factors the Court may consider in deciding your custody case: § 14-10-124, § 14-10-129, § 14-10-131, C.R.S.

RELOCATION

If you want to relocate with your children to another state or a city that will make your parenting plan impossible to maintain, you need to file a motion requesting the Court allow you to relocate the children. If you move and do not do this, you may get your kids taken away.

When determining whether to allow a parent to relocate, the Court considers the best interest factors under § 14-10-124 enumerated above along with some additional factors:

- The reasons why the party wishes to relocate with the child;
- The reasons why the opposing party is objecting to the proposed relocation;
- The history and quality of each party's relationship with the child since any previous parenting time order;
- The educational opportunities for the child at the existing location and at the proposed new location;
- The presence or absence of extended family at the existing lo-

cation and at the proposed new location;
- Any advantages of the child remaining with the primary caregiver;
- The anticipated impact of the move on the child;
- Whether the court will be able to fashion a reasonable parenting time schedule if the change requested is permitted; and
- Any other relevant factors bearing on the best interests of the child; or

Judges dread deciding relocation cases because they have to choose a winner and a loser instead of ordering essentially a compromise like they do in custody cases. I have seen these cases come out both ways and the best advice I can give you is, make sure you tell the Court why your position is in your children's best interest. I cannot stress this enough. When the court feels like one parent is making the case all about their rights or why the relocation is good for themselves, the Courts tend to go the other way. Also, if you argue that relocation is good for the kids because they don't really like the other parent, that tends to backfire because the Court does not want to take the kids away from an already strained relationship. Courts like to hear about continuity with the child's community and family.

Do not abscond with your child to another state and then try to modify. The UCCJEA under § 14-13-301, et seq. allows the Court to issue a warrant for your arrest and to take your child into custody and return the child to the other parent if you do this. This would be terribly traumatic for your child. If you feel you need to run for your safety or the safety of your child, there are other things you can do. Contact a shelter; file a protection order; consult with an attorney to discuss all your options. Courts tend to view parents who abscond unfavorably and this could backfire on you even if you had good intentions.

Remember, one of you is asking the Court to essentially remove the children from the other parent. This is a high burden of proof. You may consider running your facts by an attorney in a legal aid clinic to get their impressions of the weaknesses and strengths in your case in order to help you better prepare.

GRANDPARENT VISITATION

The law gives deference to parents' decisions as to whom their children spend time with. In 2000, the United States Supreme Court ruled in *Troxel v. Granville*[1] that parents have a Constitutional right under the Fourteenth Amendment to direct the care, custody and control of their children, and that this includes their rights to keep grandparents from seeing them. With *Troxel* also came into law an automatic presumption that a parent's decision is in the best interests of the child. Colorado Courts have repeatedly upheld this ruling.

Under § 19-1-117, C.R.S., a grandparent may seek a visitation order when there has been a child custody case, which the statute defines as follows:

1. That the marriage of the child's parents has been declared invalid or has been dissolved by a court or that a court has entered a decree of legal separation with regard to such marriage;
2. That legal custody of or parental responsibilities with respect

to the child have been given or allocated to a party other than the child's parent or that the child has been placed outside of and does not reside in the home of the child's parent, excluding any child who has been placed for adoption or whose adoption has been legally finalized; or

3. That the child's parent, who is the child of the grandparent, has died.

If there is no endangerment and there are no prior custody orders, there is no way for grandparents to get a court order for visitation[2].

Grandparents seeking visitation under § 19-1-117, C.R.S. must prove by clear and convincing evidence the following[3]:

1. that the parents' determination is not in the child's best interests.
2. that the visitation schedule they seek is in the child's best interests.

The "clear and convincing evidence" standard is one of the highest standards and can be a tough burden of proof. What this basically means is you must come prepared with solid evidence.

If there has never been a custody order concerning the grandchildren, grandparents' only remedy to seek a court order giving them time with the children is typically a guardianship over the grandchildren. In order to obtain a guardianship, grandparents must be able to prove to the Court that the current home of the children is unfit in some way (such as the parents are drug users or hoarders, or there is neglect). If there is no endangerment, grandparents will likely not be successful in obtaining guardianship over the children. Grandparents also have the option of reporting endangerment to the Department of Human Services (DHS). If DHS investigates and believes the children are in danger, DHS can open a child protection case in Court, where grandparents may request placement of the children.

STEPPARENT ADOPTION AND TERMINATION

If you are asking the court to allow your new spouse to adopt your child and to terminate the other parent's parental rights you have to show that the other parent either has not paid adequate child support for a year or more or that the other parent has abandoned the child for a year or more. If a court has addressed child support but declined to order child support, you cannot show that the other parent has failed to pay child support because there is no child support order and the court has already considered it. But if the court has never addressed child support or there's a child support order but the parent has not paid the full amount for a year, then you can show that the parent has failed to adequately support the child.

There is no statutory definition for abandonment. And you may be able to show abandonment even if there has been a little bit of contact for a year. Abandonment is subjective and will depend on the circumstances of your unique case. In one case, a parent had not seen her children in about three years, did not call on birthdays, did not ever send Christmas presents or birthday presents, but did call the children about three times a year and talk to them. The court found that there had been abandonment because this is not a meaningful parent-child relationship. In another case where a parent had not seen the child for over a year, but had tried to call the child every day even though the child did not want to talk to that parent, the court found no abandonment and instead found the custodial parent had alienated the other parent causing the child to not want to talk to them.

To file a stepparent adoption, you need to file a Petition for Stepparent Adoption and a Petition to Terminate Parental Rights. These will be heard in the same case, but you must file both requests. After you file these, you must have the other parent personally served and then file proof of service with the court, at which time the court will either schedule a hearing or a status conference. Courts don't usually order these cases to mediation because there is really no middle ground in which to settle.

Your burdens of proof are simple: one year of abandonment and/or one year of inadequate child support. You may choose to show this with text messages, phone records, support records and pictures. Also, if your child is 12 years or older, your child must consent to the adoption by signing a consent form that you will submit to the court. Your child will not be brought in to testify. However, if there is a question as to whether the child was coerced into signing the consent it is possible the judge would bring the child in to talk to them privately outside the presence of the parents.

Lastly, don't forget that the Court will want to hear from the stepparent adopting so plan on having that person testify in court as to their special relationship with the child.

Review the laws under § 19-5-201 through $19-5-203 as well as jurisdiction requirements.

PROTECTION ORDERS HEARINGS

The moment you file a motion for a protection order you get to appear before a judge because these are considered emergencies.

For the Temporary Protection Order, you will have the burden of proving that your life or health are in imminent danger.

The judge will have you explain under oath what happened, and if the judge believes your life or health are in imminent danger based on your allegations alone, the judge will issue the temporary protection order and set the matter for a permanent protection order hearing to take place within the next 14 days. In that time, you will have the other party served. See the section on Service of Process in Chapter 1 for the ways to do this.

The next step will be the Permanent Protection Order Hearing, where you and the other party will both appear at a trial. You will present testimony and evidence as to the events you alleged happened. Then the other side has the option to cross examine you and any witnesses you had testify. The other side may also choose to testify and present witnesses and evidence.

Afterwards, the judge will decide whether you have met your burden of proof and whether to issue a permanent protection order.

<u>For the Permanent Protection Order, your burden is to prove that, absent a protection order, the events alleged are likely to continue or to occur again.</u>

A good way to prove this is to show that the other person has repeatedly done the bad act despite you repeatedly asking them to stop, and perhaps even violated the temporary protection order. This shows a willful disregard for the protection order and your wishes and can be compelling evidence for you.

In a nutshell, a protection order case will usually go like this.

- Draft Verified Complaint for Protection Order, Affidavit regarding Children, Information Sheet to Register a Protection Order, Incident Checklist, and proposed Temporary Protection Order.
- Deliver the above to the Court and wait in hallway for judge to call you in.
- Testify before a judge same day as filing regarding alleged events.
- Judge either grants or denies request for temporary protection order.
- If granted, you get copy of Temporary Protection Order for yourself, and copy to have served on other party. You will schedule the Permanent Protection Order Hearing at that time, which date and time will be written on the Temporary Protection Order.
- Have other party personally served by process server with all papers filed and the Court Ordered Temporary Protection Order.
- Trial on Permanent Protection Order, where both parties appear and present evidence.

Remember, a protection order is a piece of paper and is not bullet proof. If you are in a position to need a protection order, I recommend contacting a domestic violence advocacy group to help you formulate a safety plan to ensure that you have all the safeguards in place for yourself and your children.

CONTEMPT

If you're the type of person who calls yourself a "savage" and thinks you can handle jail with the cool of Red in Shawshank Redemption, then thumbing your nose at court orders may be the thing for you. For the rest of you, know that contempt is a very serious offense for which the Court will have no hesitation about throwing you in jail, so you should probably just comply with court orders.

Contempt, by definition, means "not in compliance with court orders." If you are found by the court to be in contempt, you can face jail, a fine, or both.

There are several instances in family law where you could be found to be in contempt:

- Failure to pay maintenance;
- Failure to pay child support;
- Failure to submit disclosures;
- Failure to submit discovery responses;
- Failure to comply with the mandatory injunction under § 14-10-107, C.R.S.;
- Failure to follow the case management order;
- Failure to follow any other order.

If you are the defendant in a contempt action, you may qualify for court-appointed counsel, so make sure to inquire about this. If you believe you are truly innocent of the Contempt, do not get cocky and assume you will prevail. Take this seriously because you may be mistaken. Prepare thoroughly and obtain counsel if possible.

The process of a contempt action is as follows: You will file a motion for citation for contempt with the proposed citation and proposed order. You do not have the other party served with these! Just file them with the Court. The court will either grant or deny the motion. If granted, the court will sign the order. The Order directs the Clerk of Court to issue a citation to the other party to appear at an Advisement Hearing to plead guilty or not guilty. You will get back the signed order and signed citation. You will then have the motion, signed citation and signed order served on the other party. You will both appear at the Advisement Hearing where the other party will be asked to enter a guilty or not-guilty plea. If the other party pleads not guilty, the court will set this for a Contempt Hearing. If the other party pleads guilty, the court will sentence him at the Advisement Hearing.

At the Contempt Hearing, you will present testimony and evidence, if you have any, as to the events you alleged happened. Then the other side has the option to cross examine you and any witnesses you had testify. The party charged with the contempt may also choose to testify and present witnesses and evidence, but may also choose to plead the 5th, meaning they may choose not to testify. If you call them to testify, they have the option of pleading the 5th on every question you ask. Contempt often carries with it criminal penalties, so that is why they have the option of pleading the 5th.

In a nutshell, a contempt case will usually go like this.

- Draft Verified Motion for Citation for Contempt, Proposed Citation for Contempt, and Proposed Order Granting Motion.
- File the above with the Court.
- Judge either grants or denies motion for citation for contempt.
- If granted, judge issues Citation for Contempt commanding the other party to show up at a scheduled date and time for an Advisement Hearing. (An advisement hearing is where the other party will either plead guilty or not guilty.)
- Have other party personally served by process server with motion and the Citation and Order that were issued by the court related to the contempt.
- Appear at Advisement Hearing
- If other side pleads guilty, he will be sentenced right then. If he pleads not guilty, the Court will set a Contempt Hearing.
- Contempt Hearing where both parties appear and present evidence.

Contempt actions are governed by C.R.C.P. 107.

CHAPTER 5: DRAFT A TRIAL PLAN.

A trial plan is the roadmap of your case. It tells you where you are, where you are going, and how to get there in the most efficient and organized way possible. It will also tell you how to avoid pitfalls and dangers along the way. Without a trial plan, you will wander aimlessly through your case and have a very difficult time reaching your desired destination.

In this chapter, I provide a form for you to use so you can create your own trial plan. To start, you must lay out what you know at the beginning of your case to help you figure out what additional information you need to gather during the pendency of your case in order to prevail at the end of your case. Continuously updating the trial plan will help you organize the law and facts so you will know how to present your case. It will also help you figure out what you've got working for you and against you.

Each step of the trial plan is the foundation of a particular part of your case. For example, the Facts Beyond Dispute are what you will use to draft a cross examination. The Relevant Law will tell you what your burden of proof is, and what facts you need to make sure to bring out through testimony, witnesses or evidence. The Issues tell you what law to look up.

The first thing you need to figure out is, what are the issues in your case? Typically, a divorce case will involve the following issues: 1) division of assets, 2) division of debts, 3) child custody (allocation of parenting time and decision making), 4) child support, 5) maintenance (also called spousal support), and 6) attorney fees. Typically, a child custody case will involve 1) allocation of parenting time (the days you each have the child), 2) allocation of decision-making responsibility, and 3) child support.

Within these issues, there will be several factors unique to your case: incomes, whether one person is the primary caregiver, whether someone has squandered assets in contemplation of divorce... and so on. These over-arching issues will help you to determine what laws apply, and help you organize your trial plan by determining what evidence you have and what you need.

The following is the template to use in drafting your trial plan, and the reason and value for each section.

- **Issues:** List the issues in your case. Custody? Child Support? Maintenance?
- **Relief Requested and Reason:** What are you asking for and what are the reasons why you're asking for it?
- **Reason for dispute:** What are the reasons the other party does not agree with you? List the reasons, as this will help you prepare to defend against them.
- **Relevant law:** You need to know the standard the court will apply when deciding your case. Start with looking at the law that governs what you are asking for so you will then know where your facts fit in, if they are relevant, and what else you need to be prepared for.
- **Relevant facts (witness, evidence):** These are the things the other party may dispute, but you have evidence or witnesses that can help you prove these. List facts, not argument.
- **Facts beyond dispute:** What are the facts relevant to your case that cannot be disputed? These are facts that neither party can deny (e.g.: there are 7 days in a week, the sky is blue, other parent has been arrested, your dog bit a person). List the facts

that are good <u>and</u> bad for you.

- **Need to know:** List additional information you need to completely prepare your case.
- **Potential Witnesses:** List all potential witnesses you need to tell the Court what you want the Court to know. Witness selection will be discussed in great detail in Chapter 8.
- **Next steps (Disclosures and discovery I need):** List your action steps to get what you need to know. This will ensure your case always moves forward.

TIP: Keep the rhetoric out of your trial plan. Example: "He's a liar… he is just trying to get back at me … he tries to alienate me." There's no substance to any of this. It's argument. Keep your trial plan to facts. HOW does he try to alienate you. Be specific. Tell stories using who, what, when, where, why, how: On ___ day, he said ___ to the kids, which this witness heard, while getting in the car at Safeway.

Here is that same template filled in with sample information and explanations. (*Lawyer disclaimer – this may not apply exactly to your case, and any similarity between this and your case is pure coincidence. I'm a lawyer, not a mind-reader*).

- **Issues**: *Modifying Parenting time.*
- **Relief Requested and Reason:** *I want to modify parenting time because he is drinking too much, and he moved to Fort Collins.*
- **Reason for dispute:** *He does not want to modify parenting time because he wants the kids as much as he has them now – 50/50.*
- **Relevant law:** *14-10-129, C.R.S. Modification of Parenting Time.*

- *Court can modify if in best interests of child.*
  - *Can't file modification if less than 2 years passed since someone last filed a motion to modify asking for change in primary caregiver.*
  - *Court can't modify prior order that substantially changes parenting time and majority caregiver unless certain factors are met;*
    - *Majority parent is relocating. Court must consider the following:*
      - ◊ *Reasons why relocating with child;*
      - ◊ *Reasons opposing party objects;*
      - ◊ *history and quality of each party's relationship the child;*
      - ◊ *educational opportunities at existing and new locations;*
      - ◊ *extended family at both locations;*
      - ◊ *advantages of remaining with primary caregiver;*
      - ◊ *impact of move on child;*
      - ◊ *parenting plan possibilities;*
      - ◊ *other relevant factors.*
- 14-10-124, C.R.S. Best interest of child factors.
  - *The wishes of the child's parents as to parenting time;*
  - *The wishes of the child if he or she is sufficiently mature to express reasoned and independent preferences as to the parenting time schedule;*
  - *The interaction and interrelationship of the child with his or her parents, his or her siblings, and any other person who may significantly affect the child's best interests;*
  - *The child's adjustment to his or her home, school, and community;*
  - *The mental and physical health of all individuals involved, except that a disability alone shall not be a basis to deny or re-*

strict parenting time;

- *The ability of the parties to encourage the sharing of love, affection, and contact between the child and the other party; except that, if the court determines that a party is acting to protect the child from witnessing domestic violence or from being a victim of child abuse or neglect or domestic violence, the party's protective actions shall not be considered with respect to this factor;*
- *Whether the past pattern of involvement of the parties with the child reflects a system of values, time commitment, and mutual support;*
- *The physical proximity of the parties to each other as this relates to the practical considerations of parenting time;*
- *The ability of each party to place the needs of the child ahead of his or her own needs.*

- **Relevant facts:**

  - *Sally saw him drinking at the bar with the kids,*
  - *My mom overheard him say he only wants parenting time so he doesn't have to pay child support,*
  - *My daughter says she is scared of him when he drinks,*
  - *My daughter's teacher thinks he's Dad of the Year,*
  - *He regularly posts pictures on social media of drinking on his parenting time,*
  - *He will accuse me of alienation,*
  - *I am the primary caregiver. I take our child to all doctor appointments and attend all parent-teacher conferences. We are more bonded than he is with our child. He will probably dispute this;*
  - *We have family here in town. We have no family in Fort Collins;*
  - *Child cannot possibly be driven to and from school from Fort*

Collins because school is in Douglas county;
- ○ *Child will miss dad. This will be hard on him not seeing him every week;*
- ○ *Child would miss me more if he had to go live with his dad though;*
- ○ *Child and dad do a lot together: go fishing, play baseball, and video games*
- ○ *He's had two DUIs (public records);*
- ○ *My dog bit our son last year;*
- ○ *I travel often for work;*
- ○ *I used to smoke pot;*
- ○ *He was arrested for domestic abuse 5 years ago (but never charged);*
- ○ *He lives 25 miles from child's school;*
- ○ *I have emails of his abusive language;*
- ○ *My son is very involved in sports and neighborhood friends;*
- ○ *My son can bike to his grandparents' house from my house.*

- **Facts beyond dispute:**
  - ○ *He regularly posts pictures on social media of drinking on his parenting time;*
  - ○ *We have family here in town. We have no family in Fort Collins;*
  - ○ *He's had two DUIs (public records);*
  - ○ *My dog bit our son last year;*
  - ○ *I travel often for work;*
  - ○ *I used to smoke pot and he will bring that up;*
  - ○ *Fort Collins is 93 miles from daughter's school;*
  - ○ *I have emails of his abusive language.*

- **Need to know:**
  - ○ *What routes are there from his house to school? Exact drive*

  time?
  - *Will Sally testify for me?*
  - *How do I get in my child's statements since they are hearsay?*
  - *How do I get the Facebook pics into evidence?*
  - *What are the schools like at both locations?*
  - *How is he proposing we get to 50/50 parenting time?*
  - *Why does he want to relocate?*
  - *What does my son want?*

- **Potential Witnesses:**
  - *My mom and dad;*
  - *Neighbors: Jim, Susan, Andy, Christine;*
  - *Sally;*
  - *CFI (to tell court what our son wants, if he wants to stay with me).*

- **Next Steps** (Disclosures and discovery I need):
  - *Think about asking court to appoint Child and Family Investigator. If I can have a CFI back me up, I may have a better chance of prevailing;*
  - *Run CBI Background Check on him;*
  - *Run Court background Check;*
  - *Map routes to/from school to his house;*
  - *Print social media pages;*
  - *Ask witnesses to testify as to son's friendships with their kids; ask family to testify as to son's and my relationship, involvement with them, in community, in school, observations with his dad; talk to Sally;*
  - *Figure out how I'll deal with travel and school drop off if dad moves to Fort Collins;*
  - *Research school ratings;*
  - *Discuss potential parenting plan options with the ex.*

When you draft this trial plan, it will start off small, but you will inevitably add to it regularly, or at least you should. This sample is by no means comprehensive. My trial plans can grow to pages and pages long. You want to be sure you hit every burden of proof that you have under the law.

In the sample above, a mother is seeking a modification of parenting time. There are concerns of potential alcohol abuse around the children, which is an endangerment issue, so she needs to gather evidence to support this very serious allegation. It sounds like the father is relocating to a city which will make the parenting plan difficult to continue anyway, and the Court may treat that case like a relocation due to the distance.

Here is an abbreviated example of a multi-issue trial plan:

- **Issues**: *Divorce: Custody, asset division, debt division, maintenance, child support.*
- **Relief Requested and Reason:** *I want majority parenting time and Ex to have every other weekend; 50/50 split of assets and debts; maintenance for however long the law says I get it; child support.*
- **Reason for dispute:** *Ex wants 50/50 custody; agrees to 50/50 split of assets and debts but doesn't agree on value of some things; says he'll see me in hell before he pays a dime of maintenance; doesn't think he should have to pay child support if we have 50/50.*
- **Relevant law:**
    - *14-10-113 (division of property);*
    - *14-10-114 (maintenance), [need to know incomes of us both];*
    - *14-10-115 (child support) [need to know incomes of us both, including bonuses and incoming money from every source;*

how much our children's portion of the health insurance is; what are the average monthly daycare costs];
- *14-10-124 (best interests of child).*

There are a lot of laws listed here to paraphrase, so I kept this brief. You will want to read all the relevant laws and list out everything you believe is relevant and what your burden of proof is. I suggest writing down the parts of these statutes and any relevant case law cited at the end of the statutes that you believe may be relevant to your case.

- **Relevant facts:**
    - *Assets: each has a 401(k); house, 2 cars, bank accounts, window business, gun collection;*
    - *Debts: 2 credit cards and loan from Uncle Steve;*
    - *Incomes: not sure what his is;*
    - *Kids: Daisy and Jon, ages 2, 4.*
- **Facts beyond dispute:**
    - *Marriage is irretrievably broken;*
    - *We have 2 kids;*
    - *Been married 10 years;*
    - *I have lived in Colorado for at least 91 days before filing;*
    - *We agree on values of cars and 401(k)s;*
    - *Daycare costs $750 a month for Daisy and $500 for Jon.*
- **Need to know:**
    - *Values of accounts;*
    - *balance of debts;*
    - *exact incomes, Does he get bonuses? Overtime?*
    - *value of house;*
    - *value of business;*

- *Value of gun collection;*
- *Health insurance cost for kids for child support calculation.*

- **Potential Witnesses**
  - *My mom and dad;*
  - *Neighbors: Jim, Susan, Andy, Christine;*
  - *Sally;*
  - *CFI (to tell court what our son wants if he wants to stay with me).*

- **Next Steps** (Disclosures and discovery I need):
  - *pay stubs;*
  - *business financials;*
  - *Kelly Blue Book value of cars;*
  - *bank statements;*
  - *401(k) statements;*
  - *debt statements;*
  - *find gun appraiser;*
  - *find home appraiser;*
  - *find business valuation expert*
  - *insurance docs showing child portion.*

TIP: If the insurance documentation does not differentiate the cost between the child's portion and the other insureds, § 14-10-115(1)(c) requires you calculate this by taking the total amount of insurance premium and divide it by the number of those covered to get a per-person amount. Then you can multiply that times the number of children.

Starting your trial plan early helps you determine what your next steps are. In the first examples, this party realizes she may want the Court to appoint a Child and Family Investigator to address the child hearsay and needs to do a lot of preparation including running background checks. Since you will have to disclose any evidence you intend to use in advance, you will want to start getting it trial-ready now.

In the second example, this party realizes she does not know anything about her case yet: value of business, value of house or financial accounts. Financial disclosures will answer some questions such as values of financial accounts and incomes of parties. However, you may want to seek to appoint an expert to determine other relevant matters.

The trial plan is a work in progress. It should be updated regularly to ensure you're on track gathering what you need to adequately prepare your case. Remember to add all the facts, not just the ones that help you. You must consider the bad facts against you. Be honest with yourself when drafting this. For example, if you are planning on accusing the other parent of neglecting your child's dental care which resulted in your child needing an insane amount of dental work as a result, don't forget that child had two parents. Some accusations may backfire on you.

Also, as you learn information about the ex, adding to the trial plan will help you figure out what new information you need. For example, if you learn he blew $15,000 of marital money on jewelry for his new flame, you will want to ask the court to apportion a more favorable offset of assets to you so you don't end up paying half of that purchase. Also, people tend to be more honest about disclosing their full income on loan documentation, so if your ex bought a new vehicle in the last three years, be sure to get those loan applications you are entitled to in the initial disclosures so you can see what they reported as their income!

Now that you have your trial plan, you can start the process of gathering information for trial!

CHAPTER 6: DISCLOSURES AND DISCOVERY

In every domestic case involving financial issues (maintenance, child support, division of assets/debts), the parties are required to exchange financial disclosures.

Disclosures refer to mandatory information and documents you must share by a certain deadline. The purpose of doing this is to place the parties on equal footing, to ensure both sides have the same information to resolve the case. Disclosures in a family law case consist of mandatory financial disclosures and witness disclosures.

Discovery refers to optional requests for additional information and documents above and beyond what you already are entitled to in disclosures. You may not send requests for discovery until after you have had your Initial Status Conference.

WITNESS DISCLOSURES

You must disclose your potential witnesses well in advance of trial. Gone are the days of trial by surprise. Witness disclosures must be filed no later than 63 days before trial, and if you have an expert, your expert must prepare a report containing all their findings and testimony they will offer at trial, or the expert cannot testify to that material. This must be disclosed to the other party no later than 56 days before trial.

Witness disclosures are a captioned document that lists your witnesses' names (including yourself), phone numbers and addresses, and a brief description of what they will testify to. You will also want to preserve your right to disclose any witnesses you think of later, so be sure to include the general language in the sample:

[CAPTION]

Petitioner Jason Thorne, hereby discloses the following lay witnesses and expert witnesses that he intends to call to testify at the Motion to Modify Child Support hearing scheduled for April 16, 2023 at 10:00 AM, pursuant to C.R.C.P. Rule 16.2(e)(3):

LAY WITNESSES

1. Petitioner Jason Thorne, 567 Passport Lane, Evergreen, CO. 80437, (720) 555-1234, may testify regarding any evidence pertaining to the allegations asserted in this matter.
2. Respondent Marie Fischer, 363 Accomplice Ave, Superior, CO. 80027, (303) 555-9876 may testify regarding any evidence pertaining to the allegations asserted in this matter.
3. Pamela Shandy, 2468 Skyscraper Dr., Arvada, CO 80031, (303) 555-9753, may testify regarding Respondent's marketing efforts, stated desires regarding work and marketing, her own observations as to Respondent's efforts to obtain work.
4. Any person endorsed by either party.
5. Any person necessary for rebuttal or impeachment.
6. Any person identified during the course of discovery.
7. Any person identified in any document produced by any party in this matter.
8. Any person necessary to lay foundation or authenticate a document

EXPERT WITNESSES

9. Ward Ammond with Supreme Real Estate, 6020 Germany

Blvd., Ste. 1000, Greenwood Village, CO. 80111, (303) 555-2000, may testify as to the real estate market between the years of 2019 to present, marketing strategies to build business as a real estate agent in the current market, and Respondent's marketing efforts and sales potential. Mr. Abbott's expert report and CV are submitted with this disclosure.

10. Any person identified during the course of discovery.
11. Any person identified in any document produced by any party in this matter.
12. Any person necessary to lay foundation or authenticate a document

Respectfully submitted on January 10, 2020.

If the other side discloses an expert and expert report, you may retain a rebuttal expert. The rebuttal expert must be disclosed, and the report provided, no later than 35 days before trial.

Think twice before you decide to select a witness who may be adverse to you. You may be tempted to call your ex's sister to testify for you because she witnessed some of their bad behavior. The flaw in this plan is that it fails to consider she is their sister and may feel an undying loyalty to them and be willing to twist the facts in their favor. Calling potentially adverse witnesses is risky. Try instead to think of witnesses you are sure will not turn on you. Make sure to make notes of potentially good and bad witnesses in your trial plan.

The details of these rules can be found in C.R.C.P. 16.2(e)(3) and 16.2(g). There is not a JDF form for witness disclosures, so you will have to draft it yourself.

FINANCIAL DISCLOSURES

Financial disclosures consist of a Sworn Financial Statement, supporting documents, and a Certificate of Compliance.

The Sworn Financial Statement is a captioned form where you list your income, expenses, assets and debts. The purpose of this is to give the other party and the Court a snapshot of the entire financial picture at issue in your case so the court can equitably divide assets and debts, and calculate maintenance or child support based on the incomes and needs of the parties. Financial disclosures should be updated throughout the case as changes occur and should be updated within 6 weeks before trial.

The supporting documentation backs up the figures listed on the Sworn Financial Statement and generally consists of three years of tax returns and W-2s, pay stubs, and the most recent statement for all accounts (bank, debt, insurance of all types, investments, and so on).

The Sworn Financial Statement refers to both the JDF 1111 and JDF 1111SS. Here is what it looks like:

<table>
<tr><td>☐District Court ☐Denver Juvenile Court
________________ County, Colorado
Court Address:

In re:
☐The Marriage of:
☐The Civil Union of:
☐Parental Responsibilities concerning:
____
Petitioner:

and

Co-Petitioner/Respondent:</td><td>COURT USE ONLY</td></tr>
<tr><td>Attorney or Party Without Attorney (Name and Address):

Phone Number: E-mail:
FAX Number: Atty. Reg. #:</td><td>Case Number:

Division
Courtroom</td></tr>
<tr><td colspan="2">SWORN FINANCIAL STATEMENT</td></tr>
</table>

I, ______________________________ (full name) ❑am ❑am not currently employed.

I am employed ____ hours per week. I am paid ❑weekly ❑bi-weekly ❑twice a month ❑monthly.

My pay is based on a ❑Monthly Salary ❑Hourly rate of $__________ ❑Other: ____________________

Date employment began ______________________.

My occupation is: ____________________ Name of employer: ______________________

Address of employer: ____

If unemployed, what date did you last work? ________________

I am unemployed due to ❑disability ❑involuntary layoff at work ❑other: ______________________

This household consists of _____ adult(s), and ______ minor child(ren).

I believe the monthly gross income of the other party is $___________.

Annual gross income (last tax year 20__) for Petitioner $ _________, ❑Co-Petitioner/Respondent $ __________

1. Monthly Income (Convert annual, bi-monthly, and weekly amounts to monthly amounts.)

Gross Monthly Income (before taxes and deductions) from salary and wages, including commissions, bonuses, overtime, self-employment, business income, other jobs, and monthly reimbursed expenses.	$	Social Security Benefits (SSA) ☐SSDI (Disability insurance – entitlement program) ☐SSI (supplemental income – need based)	$
Unemployment & Veterans' Benefits		Disability, Workers' Compensation	
Pension & Retirement Benefits		Interest & Dividends	
Public Assistance (TANF)		Other - ____________	
Total Monthly Income			$
Miscellaneous Income			
Royalties, Trusts, and Other Investments	$	Contributions from Others	$
Dependent Children's monthly gross income. Source of Income: ________		All other sources, i.e. personal injury settlement, non-reported income, etc.	
Rental Net Income		Expense Accounts	
Child Support from Others		Other - ____________	
Spousal/Partner Support from Others		Other - ____________	
Total Monthly Miscellaneous Income			$
Total Income			$

2. Monthly Deductions (Mandatory and Voluntary)

Mandatory Deductions	Cost Per Month		Cost Per Month
Federal Income Tax	$	State/Local Income Tax	$
PERA/Civil Service		Social Security Tax	
Medicare Tax		Other -	
		Total Mandatory Deductions	$
Voluntary Deductions	Cost Per Month		Cost Per Month
Life and Disability Insurance	$	Stocks/Bonds	$
Health, Dental, Vision Insurance Premium Total number of people covered on Plan ➔		Retirement & Deferred Compensation	
Child Care (deducted from salary)		Other - ____________________	
Flex Benefit Cafeteria Plan		Other - ____________________	
		Total Voluntary Deductions	$
		Total Monthly Deductions	$

3. Monthly Expenses

Note: List regular monthly expenses below that you pay on an on-going basis and that are not identified in the deductions above.

A. Housing

	Cost Per Month		Cost Per Month
1st Mortgage	$	2nd Mortgage	$
Insurance (Home/Rental) & Property Taxes (not included in mortgage payment)		Condo/Homeowner's/Maintenance Fees	
Rent		Other - ______	
		Total Housing	**$**

B. Utilities and Miscellaneous Housing Services

	Cost Per Month		Cost Per Month
Gas & Electricity	$	Water, Sewer, Trash Removal	$
Telephone (local, long distance, cellular & pager)		Property Care (Lawn, snow removal, cleaning, security system, etc.)	
Internet Provider, Cable & Satellite TV		Other - ______	
		Total Utilities and Miscellaneous Housing Services	**$**

C. Food & Supplies

	Cost Per Month		Cost Per Month
Groceries & Supplies	$	Dining Out	$
		Total Food & Supplies	**$**

D. Health Care Costs (Co-pays, Premiums, etc.)

	Cost Per Month		Cost Per Month
Doctor & Vision Care	$	Dentist and Orthodontist	$
Medicine & RX Drugs		Therapist	
Premiums (if not paid by employer)		Other - ______	
		Total Health Care	**$**

E. Transportation & Recreation Vehicles (Motorcycles, Motor Homes, Boats, ATV, Snowmobiles, etc.)

	Cost Per Month		Cost Per Month
Primary Vehicle Payment	$	Other Vehicle Payments	$
Fuel, Parking, and Maintenance		Insurance & Registration/Tax Payments (yearly amount(s) ÷12)	
Bus & Commuter Fees		Other - ______________	
		Total Transportation	**$**

F. Children's Expenses and Activities

	Cost Per Month		Cost Per Month
Clothing & Shoes	$	Child Care	$
Extraordinary Expenses i.e. Special Needs, etc.		Misc. Expenses, i.e. Tutor, Books, Activities, Fees, Lunch, etc.	
Tuition		Other - ______________	
Total Children's Expenses and Activities			**$**

G. Education for you - Please identify status: ❑Full-time student ❑Part-time student

	Cost Per Month		Cost Per Month
Tuition, Books, Supplies, Fees, etc.		Other - ______________	
		Total Education	**$**

H. Maintenance (Spousal/Partner Support) & Child Support (that you pay)

	Cost Per Month		Cost Per Month
Maintenance		Child Support	
❑This family	$	❑This family	$
❑Other family		❑Other family	
Total Maintenance and Child Support			**$**

4. Debts (unsecured)

List unsecured debts such as credit cards, store charge accounts, loans from family members, back taxes owed to the I.R.S., etc. **Do not** list debts that are liens against your property, such as mortgages and car loans, because that payment is already listed as an expense above, and the total of the debt is shown elsewhere as a deduction from value where that asset is listed, such as under Real Estate or Motor Vehicles.

For name on account, "P" = Petitioner, "C/R" = Co-Petitioner or Respondent, "J" = Joint.

Name of Creditor	Account Number (last 4-digits only)	P	C/R	J	Date of Balance	Balance	Minimum Monthly Payment Required	Reason for Which Debt was Incurred
		❑	❑	❑		$	$	
		❑	❑	❑				
		❑	❑	❑				
		❑	❑	❑				
		❑	❑	❑				
		❑	❑	❑				
		❑	❑	❑				
		❑	❑	❑				
		❑	❑	❑				
		❑	❑	❑				
		❑	❑	❑				
		❑	❑	❑				
		❑	❑	❑				
		❑	❑	❑				
		❑	❑	❑				
			Unsecured Debt Balance			$	$	→Total Minimum Monthly Payment

SWORN FINANCIAL STATEMENT SUMMARY (INCOME/EXPENSES)

Total Income (from Page 1)		$ ____________	A
Total Monthly Deductions (from Page 2)		$ ____________	B
	Total Monthly Net Income (A minus B)	**$ ____________**	
Total Monthly Expenses (from Page 3)		$ ____________	C
Total Minimum Monthly Payment Required - Debts Unsecured (from Page 4)		$ ____________	D
	Total Monthly Expenses and Payments (C plus D)	**$ ____________**	

Net Excess or Shortfall (Monthly Net Income less Monthly Expenses and Payments) (+/-) $ _______

5. Assets

You MUST disclose all assets correctly. By indicating "None", you are stating affirmatively that you or the other party, do not have assets in that category. Please attach additional copies of pages 5 & 6 to identify your assets, if necessary.

If the parties are married or partners in a civil union, check under the heading Joint (J) all assets acquired during the marriage/civil union but not by gift or inheritance. Under the headings of Petitioner (P) or Co-Petitioner/Respondent (C/R), check assets owned before this marriage/civil union and assets acquired by gift or inheritance.

If the parties were NEVER married **to each other** ***or are using this form to modify child support***, list all of each party's assets under the headings of Petitioner (P) or Co-Petitioner/Respondent (C/R).

"P" = Petitioner, "C/R" = Co-Petitioner or Respondent, "J" = Joint.

A. Real Estate (Address or Property Description and Name of Creditor/ Lender) ❑None	P	C/R	J	Estimated Value as of Today Value = what you could sell it for in its current condition.	Amount Owed	Net Value/Equity (Value minus amount owed)
	❑	❑	❑	$	$	$
	❑	❑	❑			
Total				$	$	$

B. Motor Vehicles & Recreation Vehicles Including Motorcycles, ATV's, Boats, etc.) (Year, Make, Model) (Name of Creditor/Lender) ❑None	P	C/R	J	Estimated Value as of Today Value = what you could sell it for in its current condition.	Amount Owed	Net Value/Equity (Value minus amount owed)
	❑	❑	❑			
	❑	❑	❑			
Total				$	$	$

C. Cash on Hand, Bank, Checking, Savings, or Health Accounts (Name of Bank or Financial Institution) ❑None	P	C/R	J	Type of Account	Account # (last 4-digits only)	Balance as of Today
	❑	❑	❑			$
	❑	❑	❑			
Total						$

D. Life Insurance (Name of Company/Beneficiary) ❑None	P	C/R	J	Type of Policy	Face Amount of Policy	Cash Value today
	❑	❑	❑		$	$
	❑	❑	❑			
Total					$	$

E. Furniture, Household Goods, and Other Personal Property, i.e. Jewelry, Antiques, Collectibles, Artwork, Power Tools, etc. Identify Items and report in total. ❑None	P	C/R	J	Current Possession Held by			Estimated Value as of Today Value = what you could sell it for in its current condition.
				P	C/R	J	
	❑	❑	❑	❑	❑	❑	$
	❑	❑	❑	❑	❑	❑	
	❑	❑	❑	❑	❑	❑	
	❑	❑	❑	❑	❑	❑	
	❑	❑	❑	❑	❑	❑	
Total							$

F. Stocks, Bonds, Mutual Funds, Securities & Investment Accounts ❑None ❑If owned please attach JDF 1111-SS.	Total	$
G. Pension, Profit Sharing, or Retirement Funds ❑None ❑If owned please attach JDF 1111-SS.	Total	$

H. Miscellaneous Assets
❑None If you own any of the assets identified below, please check the appropriate box and attach JDF 1111-SS to report the value.

❑Business Interests	❑Stock Options	❑Money/Loans owed to you	❑IRS Refunds due to you
❑Country Club & Other Memberships	❑Livestock, Crops, Farm Equipment	❑Pending lawsuit or claim by you	❑Accrued Paid Leave (sick, vacation, personal)
❑Oil and Gas Rights	❑Vacation Club Points	❑Safety Deposit Box/Vault	❑Trust Beneficiary
❑Frequent Flyer Miles	❑Education Accounts	❑Health Savings Accounts	❑Mineral and Water Rights
❑Other - ________	❑Other - ________	❑Other - ________	❑Other - ________
		Total	$

I. Separate Property ❑None ❑If owned please attach JDF 1111-SS to identify the property and to report the value.	Total	$
Total Value/Balance of All Assets (A – I)	$	

❑ By checking this box, I am acknowledging I am filling in the blanks and not changing anything else on the form.

❑ By checking this box, I am acknowledging that I have made a change to the original content of this form.

I understand that if the information I have provided changes or needs to be updated before a final decree or order is issued by the Court, that I have a duty to provide the correct or updated information.

I understand that if I have omitted or misstated any material information, intentionally or not, the Court will have the power to enter orders to address those matters, including the power to punish me for any statements made with the intent to defraud or mislead the Court or the other party.

VERIFICATION

I declare under penalty of perjury under the law of Colorado that the foregoing is true and correct.

Executed on the ______ day of ________________, ________, at ______________________________________
(date) (month) (year) (city or other location, and state OR country

____
(printed name of Petitioner or Co-Petitioner/Respondent)

____
Signature of Petitioner or Co-Petitioner/Respondent

CERTIFICATE OF SERVICE

I certify that on ________________________ (date) a true and accurate copy of the ***SWORN FINANCIAL STATEMENT*** was served on the other party by:
❑Hand Delivery, ❑E-filed, ❑Faxed to this number: ____________________, **or**
❑By placing it in the United States mail, postage pre-paid, and addressed to the following:

To: ____
____
____

____
Your signature

JDF 1111SC R1/18 SWORN FINANCIAL STATEMENT – FORM 35.2

Case Name ________________________ **and** ________________________ **Case Number:** ________________

Supporting Schedules for Assets in Section F, G, H, and I.

Attach this supporting schedule to JDF 1111 **ONLY** if you have assets in sections F & G, any additional assets to report in section H, and/or separate property to report in section I. In addition, report totals from this document to the appropriate sections on JDF 1111.

F. Stocks, Bonds, Mutual Funds, Securities & Investment Accounts (Name of Item or Fund)	P	C/R	J	# of Shares	Account # (last 4-digits only)	Current Value as of Today
	❑	❑	❑			
	❑	❑	❑			
	❑	❑	❑			
					Total	$
G. Pension, Profit Sharing, or Retirement Funds (Defined Contribution and/or Defined Benefit Plans)	**P**	**C/R**	**J**	**Type of Plan (401K, IRA, 457, PERA, Military, etc.)**	**Account # (last 4-digits only, if applicable)**	**Current Value as of Today**
	❑	❑	❑			
	❑	❑	❑			
	❑	❑	❑			
Total						$
H. Miscellaneous Assets (Identify Type of Asset)	**P**	**C/R**	**J**			**Estimated Value as of Today**
	❑	❑	❑			
	❑	❑	❑			
	❑	❑	❑			
		Total				
I. Separate Property (Identify Type)	**P**	**C/R**	**J**			**Estimated Value as of Today**
	❑	❑	❑			
	❑	❑	❑			
	❑	❑	❑			
Total						$

JDF 1111SS SC 3/06 SUPPORTING SCHEDULES FOR ASSETS – FORM 35.3

The Certificate of Compliance is a form in which you list the documents you gave the other party. By signing it, you are certifying to the court that you disclosed the documents you were supposed to disclose. A list of the supporting documents you are required to disclose are listed in the C.R.C.P. book in the Appendix to Chapters 1 to 17A, and included here for your convenience:

Mandatory Disclosure

FORM 35.1

[Reference to C.R.C.P. 16.2(e)(2). These disclosure forms are not to be filed with the court, except as may be ordered pursuant to C.R.C.P. 16.2]

Mandatory Disclosures. (Complete and accurate copies may replace originals. "Child(ren)" refers to minor child(ren) of both parties.)

Each party shall provide:

(a) Sworn Financial Statement. A completed and signed Sworn Financial Statement using the Supreme Court approved form (Form 35.2).

(b) Income Tax Returns (Most Recent 3 Years). The personal and business federal income tax returns for the three years before filing of the petition or post-decree motion. The business returns shall be for any business in which a party has an interest entitling the party to a copy of such returns. Each return shall include all schedules and attachments, such as W-2s, 1099s, and K-1. If a return is not completed at the time of disclosure, include the documents necessary to prepare the return, such as W-2s, 1099s, and K-1s, copies of extension requests, and the estimated amount of tax payments. If a decree has been entered within the last three years, only those returns filed since entry of the decree need be provided.

(c) Personal Financial Statements (Last 3 Years). All personal financial statements, statements of assets or liabilities, and credit or loan applications prepared during the last three years. If a decree has been entered within the last three years, only those statements/applications prepared since entry of the decree need be provided.

(d) Business Financial Statements (Last 3 Years). For every business in which a party has access to financial statements, the last three fiscal years' financial statements, all year-to-date financial statements, and the same periodic financial statements for the prior two years. If a decree has been entered within the last three years, only those statements prepared since entry of the decree need be provided.

(e) Real Estate Documents. The title documents and all documents stating value of all real property in which a party has a personal or business interest. This section shall not apply to post-decree motions unless so ordered by the Court.

(f) Personal Debt. All documents creating debt, and the most recent debt statements showing the outstanding balance and payment terms. This section shall not apply to post-decree motions unless so ordered by the Court.

(g) Investments. The most recent account statements or other documents identifying each investment in which a party has any personal or business interest and stating its current value.

(h) Employment Benefits. The most recent account statements or other documents identifying each employment benefit of a party and stating the current value.

(i) Retirement Plans. The most recent documents identifying each retirement plan of which a party is a beneficiary, and stating the current value, and the Summary Plan Descriptions. This section shall not apply to post-decree motions unless so ordered by the Court.

(j) Bank/Financial Institution Accounts. The most recent account statements identifying each account of a party at banks and other financial institutions and stating the current value.

(k) Income Documentation. For each income source of a party in the current and prior calendar year, including income from employment, investment, government programs, gifts, trust distributions, prizes, and income from every other source, pay stubs, a current income statement, and the final income statement for the prior year. Each self-employed party shall provide a sworn statement of gross income, business expenses necessary to produce income, and net income for the three months before filing of the petition or post-decree motion.

(l) Employment and Education-Related Child Care Documentation. Any documents that show a party's average monthly employment-related childcare expense, including childcare expense related to the party's education and job search. This section shall apply only if child support is an issue.

(m) Insurance Documentation. All life, health, and property insurance policies and current documents that show beneficiaries, coverage, cost (including the portion payable to provide health insurance for child(ren)), and payment schedule. The section shall not apply to post-decree motions unless either so ordered by the Court or, if child support is an issue, the policy and cost information regarding the child(ren) shall be provided.

(n) Extraordinary Child(ren)'s Expense Documentation. All documents that show average monthly expense for all recurring extraordinary child(ren)'s expenses. This section shall apply only if child support is an issue.

(o) Unless so ordered by the Court, these mandatory disclosures shall not apply to post-decree motions that raise only issues of decision-making and parenting time.

This list can be overwhelming, so let me simplify it for you. It basically asks for:

- three years of tax returns (the whole filing, all supporting documents. Personal and all your businesses);
- most recent account statement for banks, investments and debts;
- Copy of any loan or credit applications you filled out in the last 3 years;
- Real estate documents that show the value of the property;
- Documents showing employment benefits (like an employment contract);
- Documents that accurately reflect your income (like pay stubs);
- Documents that accurately show your child-care monthly expense;
- Insurance documentation;
- Documentation showing costs for other extraordinary chil-

dren's expenses.

Notice that you do not have to disclose all of this if you have filed a post-decree case, so do go through the list to make sure you are disclosing only what you need to.

You can download the Sworn Financial Statement and Certificate of Compliance from the court website. You will need JDF Forms 1111, 1111SS and 1104. Each party must fill out their own disclosures.

WHAT IF THE OTHER SIDE IS HIDING ASSETS?

If you believe the other side has refused to disclose something you are positive exists, you can send a demand letter, file a motion to compel, send them written discovery requests (interrogatories and requests for production), hire a private investigator or issue a subpoena. If you suspect they are hiding assets, but you can't prove it, you need to become an investigator.

A demand letter is a letter that basically says, here is what you did, here is why it was wrong, here is what I expect you to do to make it right, here is my deadline, and here is what I'll do to you if you don't make it right. Draft this letter with the sort of kindness and professionalism you want a judge to see because I assure you it will be used against you if you use abusive language.

With discovery requests, you can go through the three years of bank statements and look at all the transfers of funds. You would be surprised what you can uncover by doing this. Transfers often reveal account numbers and wire transfers to other banks and accounts you may not know existed. You are also entitled to copies of all canceled checks for those accounts. Reviewing canceled checks may reveal checks written to other accounts in that party's name, or even hidden businesses.

You can subpoena the top banks in your geographic area for accounts in which the other party has an interest. I once uncovered over $140,000 of hidden money in undisclosed accounts by doing this.

Search the Colorado Secretary of State website for any businesses in which the other party is listed as a registered agent. Small business owners often list themselves as their own registered agent. If there are hidden businesses, there are likely bank accounts associated with those businesses. Note: being a registered agent does not mean they are a business owner. However, it is a starting point to uncovering other documents associated with that business.

Private investigators can uncover titles to vehicles and other property you may not know existed. They will provide you with a comprehensive report of all the property and income history they recovered and their resources to back it up.

DISCOVERY

Discovery is a word that refers to your right to get more information from the other side than what was provided to you in the initial disclosures. In domestic relations cases, discovery refers to depositions and written discovery (interrogatories and requests for production). Through the process of discovery, you can require the other party to answer questions under oath and produce additional documents to you.

The Colorado Supreme Court has approved pre-written interrogatories and requests for production that you can copy and paste into your own document and send to the other side. The pre-written discovery is referred to as Pattern Interrogatories and Pattern Requests for Production. You can find these on the Court website as Pattern Interrogatories (Form 35.4) and Pattern Requests for Production (Form 35.5).

In addition to sending these out, you are also allowed to add 10 more questions that you wrote yourself. These are called Non-Pattern Interrogatories and Non-Pattern Requests for Production. These must consist of a single question (rather than a multi-part question like the Pattern questions have).

Discovery is a good way to try to find out about hidden information or prepare for your hearing. It may help you anticipate the testimony of the other person. It could also help you find out the other party's real income, by requiring that person to produce three years' worth of bank statements or two years' worth of credit card statements.

The deadline to serve discovery is 63 days before your scheduled hearing. The responding party has 35 days to respond from the date you serve that party. You can serve these on the other party by mail – you do not have to have the person personally served.

If you are served with discovery, you must respond within 35 days of being served with it, or you could face having to defend against a motion to compel. You are required to answer all discovery inquiries UNLESS the request demands you disclose privileged information or is otherwise protected under C.R.C.P. 26(c).

This is Very Important: If the discovery demands **privileged** or **protected** information, you must still respond! The next section explains what is privileged and protected. Be sure to review this carefully before responding to discovery to protect yourself. However, your response to those particular questions will contain your objection rather than the answer. You must also file a motion for a protective order which states the specific interrogatory, request or question you object to and the reason you object. A sample protective order appears later in this chapter under Privileges.

You are required to supplement your discovery responses as changes occur or as you get new information.

The rules that govern discovery in domestic relations cases are C.R.C.P 16.2(f), 26, 30, 33, 34, and 121 § 1-12. I recommend reading all of these before you engage in discovery or submit your responses.

PRIVILEGES

Privileged information is information that is private as between attorney and client, doctor or therapist and client, or priest and parishioner, and also includes your Constitutional Fifth Amendment right against self-incrimination.

For example, if you are asked in discovery to disclose conversations you had when consulting with an attorney, or what the attorney's advice was to you, or any discussions you had with your therapist in the course of therapy, then you can object and refuse to disclose. If you are asked about a conversation you had with your priest in the course of obtaining advice, you can refuse to disclose.

Of course, like everything in law, there are exceptions. For the doctor-patient privilege to apply, you must have been seeking treatment. In addition, this may be considered waived if you are using confidential treatment information as a defense in the case. For the attorney-client privilege to apply, you must have been seeking legal advice. The privilege does not apply if you told the attorney you intend to commit a future crime or fraud, of if the case involves you suing your attorney for malpractice.

You also do not have to answer questions that would be protected against your Constitutional 5th Amendment right against self-incrimination. You've heard people "plead the fifth" on T.V.? This is what that refers to. Here is the actual language of the Fifth Amendment:

> *No person shall be held to answer for a capital, or otherwise infamous crime, unless on a presentment or indictment of a grand jury, except in cases arising in the land or naval forces, or in the militia, when in actual service in time of war or public danger; nor shall any person be subject for the same offense to be twice put in jeopardy of life or limb;* ***nor shall be compelled in any criminal case to be a witness against himself****, nor be deprived of life, liberty, or property, without due process of law; nor shall private property be taken for public use, without just compensation.*

I emphasized the part that applies here.

What this means to you is that you are not required to disclose anything about any potential criminal activity you are alleged to have committed. However, know that **if you refuse to answer and you assert your fifth amendment right instead, this can be used against you!** Let me explain. In criminal cases, your silence cannot be used against you. However, in civil cases (such as family law cases), it CAN be used against you. Go back and read the language again of the Fifth Amendment, above: *"... nor shall be compelled **in any criminal case** to be a witness against himself."* This Constitutional Right protects you only in criminal cases. In a criminal case, the judge instructs the jury not to make any adverse inferences against an accused who refuses to testify, in order to protect this right. However, in civil cases, the Court is allowed to find that the failure of a party to answer questions based on the privilege against self-incrimination raises a strong inference that the answers would have been unfavorable and damaging to him."[4]

So, if you are asked the question, "Describe in detail each fact or event which causes you to believe that you may be subject criminal liability or criminal prosecution at the present time or at any time in the future", or a similar question violating your privilege, you may refuse to answer. Just remember that this could result in the Court drawing the conclusion that you have something to hide.

When refusing to answer on the basis of privilege, you must state your objection in the response and state which privilege you are asserting. For example:

4 See Romero v. Dept. of Human Svcs, 417 P.3d 914 (Colo. App. 2018) for the Court's interpretation of this rule.

The Respondent objects to the extent that this request seeks information protected by the Fifth Amendment privilege under the U.S. Constitution. This request seeks to compel the Respondent to testify against himself regarding criminal matters in violation of his Fifth Amendment right against self-incrimination.

OTHER PROTECTIONS

C.R.C.P. 26(c) allows you to seek a protective order against disclosure of information to protect against annoyance, embarrassment, oppression, or undue burden or expense. When you file the motion for a protective order, you are relieved from disclosing the information you seek to protect until the court rules on your motion, under C.R.C.P. 121 § 1-12.

In your motion for a protective order, you can ask the court to order any of the following:

- That the disclosure or discovery not be had;
- That the disclosure or discovery may be had only on specified terms and conditions, including a designation of the time or place or the allocation of expenses;
- That the discovery may be had only by a method of discovery other than that selected by the party seeking discovery;
- That certain matters not be inquired into, or that the scope of the disclosure or discovery be limited to certain matters;
- That discovery be conducted with no one present except persons designated by the court;
- That a deposition, after being sealed, be opened only by order of the court;

- That a trade secret or other confidential research, development, or commercial information not be revealed or be revealed only in a designated way; and
- That the parties simultaneously file specified documents or information enclosed in sealed envelopes to be opened as directed by the court.

You must file your motion for a protective order with the court within the 35 days to respond and state your specific objection to the discovery question in your response that you send back. Your objection may look like this:

Defendant objects to this request for production as overly broad and burdensome

Here is a sample motion for protective order.

[CAPTION]

The Respondent, Bella Jahn, hereby moves the Court to issue a protective order pursuant to C.R.C.P. 26(c) on the basis that the information sought, described below, is not relevant to the issue of child support modification and is not reasonably calculated to lead to the discovery of admissible evidence, and states as follows.

AUTHORITY

1. "Parties may obtain discovery regarding any matter, not privileged, that is relevant to the claim or defense of any party." C.R.C.P. 26(b)(1) (emphasis added). "Relevant information need not be admissible at the trial if the discovery appears reasonably calculated

to lead to the discovery of admissible evidence." *Id.*

2. "Upon motion by a party and for good cause shown, the court may make any order which justice requires to protect a party or person from annoyance, embarrassment, oppression, or undue burden or expense, including that certain matters not be inquired into, or that the scope of the disclosure or discovery be limited to certain matters." C.R.C.P. 26(c).

MOTION

3. The issue pending before the court in this case is modification of child support, requested by the Petitioner Edward Mullen on the basis of a substantial and continuing change in circumstances.

4. Mr. Mullen propounded formal written discovery on Ms. Jahn, which included pattern and non-pattern requests for production of documents dating back to January 1, 2017.

5. The large scope in time of documents requested contains time-frames which are irrelevant to the matter pending before the court, because child support is only modifiable back to the date the motion was filed, and because the last child support order was as recent as August 13, 2019. For this reason, the requests are also unduly burdensome, and not reasonably calculated to lead to the discovery of admissible evidence.

6. Ms. Jahn moves the Court to enter a protective order prohibiting discovery into the matters beyond the scope of the modification period for the above stated reasons. Specifically, Ms. Jahn requests the Court order she not be required to produce responsive documents predating August 13, 2019.

WHEREFORE, the Respondent Bella Jahn respectfully moves the Court for a protective order regarding the above referenced matters limiting the responsive document production to documents including and after August 13, 2019.

SUBPOENAS

C.R.C.P. 45, the rule governing subpoenas, says you can't use subpoenas to avoid the limits of disclosure or discovery. What that means to you is that you have to try and get the information you want by asking for it first, and through the proper disclosure or discovery.

Make a note in your trial plan that you think you may need to subpoena something in particular but use it as a last resort. Document all attempts you made to obtain the information through other channels in case you are asked to explain yourself later.

The rule governing subpoenas can be found in C.R.C.P. 45.

MOTION TO COMPEL

If you do not get the disclosures or discovery you are entitled to by the deadline, you can file a motion to compel. This remedy is governed by C.R.C.P. 37, which says that if you file a motion to compel and the court finds the party did not provide what they were supposed to, the court can issue an order compelling that party to produce the information to you by a certain date and order sanctions or a fine against that party, including attorney fees in your favor for any fees incurred in trying to get that information.

To draft the motion to compel, you will simply need to state what it is you are seeking, what rule you believe it is governed by, when you were entitled to it, and what happened (e.g. they refused or failed to provide it). Before you file the motion, you must first talk with the other party and try to resolve the issue in a reasonable way. For example, email the other party and tell them you were entitled to this document under the relevant disclosure/discovery rule, and tell them if you do not get it by a date (about 7 days in advance), you will seek the assistance of the court.

> *Dear William,*
>
> *Pursuant to CRCP Rule 16.2, you were required to provide me with your most recent income documentation. I have not received any pay stubs or other documentation from you to show what your income is. Please provide this documentation to me no later than December 12. Otherwise, I will have no alternative but to seek the assistance of the court. I look forward to an amicable resolution to this issue.*
>
> *Sincerely, Kate*

Remember to always be kind and professional in your correspondence to the other side, because that correspondence may become an exhibit the judge is going to see one day.

CHAPTER 7: EXPERTS

WHY DO I NEED AN EXPERT?

There are two types of witnesses: lay witnesses and expert witnesses. Lay witnesses can testify based on their observations. Expert witnesses are used to help a judge understand something specialized that a lay witness typically would not have knowledge of, such as scientific or technical knowledge.

For example, a lay witness may testify that she has seen your ex intoxicated and describe what behaviors she observed. An expert witness may testify regarding the effects of meth on a person's ability to effectively parent while under the influence, as well as the addictive effects of the drug, and typical addictive behaviors.

A lay witness may testify that she has observed your ex's driving and that he drives (in her opinion) erratically, running red lights and speeding. She may not testify regarding statistical chances of being in an accident based on this driving behavior. This is better suited for an expert.

A lay witness may testify that she heard your ex stating he does not want to work and has called in sick when he was not ill. This witness may not, however, testify that she believes your ex is capable of earning $85,000 based on his years of experience in his field of work. This is more specialized knowledge for which you'd need an expert. Even if your friend happens to be a vocational evaluation expert, you would need to qualify your friend as an expert in this field before she can offer that specialized knowledge in testimony.

USUAL TYPES OF EXPERTS IN FAMILY LAW

CHILD AND FAMILY INVESTIGATOR

In contentious custody battles, parties may want to ask the Court to appoint a CFI, or the Court may appoint one on its own. A CFI is a neutral third party, usually a licensed attorney or mental health professional with knowledge and experience in family dynamics and child development, and sometimes also substance abuse and domestic abuse.

CFIs interview the parties, meet the children, observe the parties interacting with the children, interview the parties' references, and make recommendations to the Court as to what custody arrangement is in the best interests of the child. You may want a CFI appointed if you have concerns about the other parent's ability to properly care for the children, or you want to be the majority time parent.

At the time of writing this book, the cost of a CFI is $2,750.00 and does not include their fee to testify at trial. This fee is typically split evenly between the parties, but some courts will order one party to pay the entire cost up front and apportion the cost later at trial. If your income is low enough, you may qualify to have the state pay for your portion. You will want to inquire about this if it comes up. To apply for the state to pay your portion, you must complete a JDF 208 and submit it with your Motion for Appointment of a Child and Family Investigator (JDF 1317) and the proposed Order Appointing Child and Family Investigator (JDF 1318).

The Court publishes lists of approved CFIs for every district court, so if you want to request a CFI be appointed, go on the Court website using the URL provided in the Appendix. You will want to let the court know at the initial status conference if you want one appointed so the CFI will have the duration of the case to complete the investigation.

The statute authorizing CFIs can be found at § 14-10-116.5, C.R.S.

PARENTAL RESPONSIBILITIES EVALUATOR

A Parental Responsibilities Evaluator ("PRE") conducts a broader evaluation than a CFI and is more appropriate for cases involving substance abuse or where mental health of one of the parties is a concern. PREs are typically doctors of psychology or psychiatry. Their rates are not capped and can range from $8,000 and up. The highest I have seen a PRE cost go is $25,000 and that was in 2010. Since these are not capped, if you decide you want a PRE, you should try and negotiate a flat fee or a ceiling for the total cost.

Unfortunately, you cannot get the state to pay for a PRE for you. However, you can ask the Court to order the County Department of Human Services (DHS) to perform an evaluation and file a written report concerning the disputed issues, and ask that that cost be borne by the state or the other party.

The statute authorizing PREs and a DHS evaluation can be

found at § 14-10-127, C.R.S. If you'd like to request a PRE, you need to draft your own motion because there is not a JDF form for it. However, you can use the Motion and Proposed Order forms for a CFI as a template (JDF 1317 and 1318).

VOCATIONAL EVALUATION EXPERT

A Vocational Evaluation Expert is someone with a vocational or occupational rehabilitation background who can assess a party's skills, education, work experience, physical ability, among other things, and prepare a report summarizing the jobs that person may qualify for, employability and earning capacity. This expert comes in handy when one spouse is claiming they are unable to earn more income than you believe they are capable of earning.

Parties typically hire their own vocational evaluation experts, but you could hire a joint one. This expert does not need to be court appointed so you do not have to file a motion. You simply retain the expert yourself.

BUSINESS VALUATION EXPERT

As the title suggests, this expert values a party's ownership interest in a business. Remember, even if your spouse owned the business before you got married, the value may have increased during the course of the marriage. That increase in value is marital, and you may be entitled to assets worth a portion of that increase in value. In order to determine the increase in value, this expert may perform a present-day valuation and a retrospective valuation (as of the date of marriage) in order to determine the amount of the increase.

This expert does not need to be court appointed so you do not have to file a motion. You simply retain the expert yourself.

HOME APPRAISER

A home appraiser assesses the value of the home and provides a detailed report with the assessed value and analysis. You will likely need to have all real estate either you or your spouse own, individually or together, appraised. Like a business, even if your spouse owned a home before you got married and never added you to the title, you may still have an interest in any increase in value of the home during the course of the marriage. An appraiser can perform a present-day appraisal and a retrospective appraisal in order to determine the amount of the increase in value, if any.

This expert does not need to be court appointed so you do not have to file a motion. You simply retain the expert yourself.

OTHER EXPERTS

You can hire an expert for just about anything that you need an expert opinion on. There are experts in the field of domestic violence, real estate market and sales, tools, cars, guns, and more. I recommend turning to Google and your local legal aid clinics for assistance in finding the unique type of expert you may need.

HOW DO I PICK AN EXPERT?

There are several resources with which to find experts, depending on the type you need. One way is to ask an attorney. Attorneys in particular geographic areas tend to utilize the same people over and over as experts in their cases. So, one thing you can do is go to a free legal aid clinic and ask a lawyer who they like, and why. You can also try America's most popular research tool: Google. The Court website has a resource page as well where you can find mediators and CFIs. That URL is provided in the Free Legal Resources appendix at the end of this book. You can try a law library and ask for an expert directory. There are a few expert directories out there, and that will at least give you a starting point to look up names to google.

Lawyer opinions about experts are going to be much more reliable than internet feedback. Web reviews can be one-sided and inaccurate because they are typically written by unhappy people for whom the report or case did not come out favorably. What you want is an expert who is thorough and will uncover the truth – not one who leans more toward dads, blondes, or whatever else. Those experts have a bad reputation in the community, so even if the report did come out favorably for you, it will not be given much weight with the court.

Some experts, such as CFIs and PREs, must be appointed by the Court. For these, you must file a motion asking the Court to appoint one. This is explained further in this chapter.

Rule 16.2 requires that you try and select a joint expert with the other party, such as one home appraiser. A joint expert is someone that you two agree to perform one valuation. By agreeing to a joint expert, you are not giving up your right to contest the expert's findings. If you two cannot agree on a joint expert, then you can select an expert of your own, and the other party can then select a rebuttal expert. Under C.R.C.P. 16.2(4), the parties both have a duty to cooperate with and supply documents and other information requested by any expert. Therefore, if the other party refuses to cooperate, you may need to seek the assistance of the court in compelling their cooperation.

You may be wondering whether you need an expert in your case at all, and if so, for what. Below is a list of typical experts utilized in family law cases to assist you in determining whether one may be of assistance in your case.

SECTION 3 – TRIAL

When I was in Boot Camp, I sprained my ankle really badly about halfway through. I wasn't able to run, road march, or do various obstacle courses. Honestly, it was a nice break and I thought I had it pretty good. That was until I learned that if I couldn't pass the final Physical Training (PT) test they wouldn't let me graduate and I would have to start Boot Camp all over again from day one.

[internal scream]

There had been one girl that broke her leg right around the time I sprained my ankle. She had a cast going all the way from her foot up to the top of her thigh. They sent her home for a few months to heal and didn't let her out of the Army. So, I knew she was going to have to repeat all of this over again and my heart broke for her. Now here I was, facing the same thing.

Look, I tell everyone I loved Boot Camp, which is true - I had fun. There is a lot about it that I enjoyed. But there was just no way that I was doing it twice.

I needed to pass this test.

To pass the PT test, I had to run two miles in a certain amount of time, and I knew it would be tough because I hadn't run in weeks. To make matters worse, even before I sprained my ankle, I wasn't running fast enough to pass this PT test. And now here I was with a sprained ankle having to pass this PT test. I had to get a doctor's permission just to take the PT test.

The first time I ran after the sprain was the day of the PT test.

Now, for those of you who have been in the Army, you know that the Army's answer for anything, from a headache to a missing limb, is Motrin. So, following this sage medical advice, I popped two Motrins and ran my heart out. The last quarter mile of the run I was in excruciating pain and crying. My company commander saw I was struggling and so he came up and ran beside me the whole way in for the last quarter mile, encouraging me all the way. I crossed the finish line with time to spare, tears streaming down my face, and my ankle screaming at me. But I did it!

Trial is not that different. No matter how much you prepare, something is going to happen that's going to throw you off and surprise you. I've literally never walked out of court and thought to myself, "wow, that went exactly like I thought it would go." Just know it's going to happen and accept it. You worked hard all this time, prepared really well, and now you're at the final test. Even though you may be running on a sprained ankle, you will get through this, as tough and daunting as it is. You will do great because you've learned that you can push yourself.

CHAPTER 8: PRETRIAL PREPARATION

Once you get a trial date, the first thing you must do is calendar the pretrial deadlines that are listed in Chapter 3 of this book. Then you will begin preparing your case for trial.

This is where your trial plan that we discussed in Chapter 5 will begin to come in handy. As you have gathered and reviewed disclosures and discovery, and reviewed expert reports and valuation reports, you can begin to figure out how to present all that information to a judge.

Information is presented to a judge through witnesses. You are a witness in your own case. You may also have other people as witnesses. Through witness testimony, you will introduce evidence. You will figure out who to call as a witness from your trial plan. With your trial plan, you will figure out which witnesses can authenticate which documents.

I'm sure this sounds overwhelming but if you are organized and prepare in advance, you will see it comes together very easily. This chapter will assist you in figuring out how to organize that information to effectively present it to the Court.

PLANNING FOR THE TIMING OF YOUR CASE

If you are set for a 3-hour trial, that means you and the other side each have less than an hour and a half to present your case. Presenting your case includes: 1) your opening statement, 2) your closing argument, 3) your testimony, 4) questioning your witnesses, 3) cross examining the other side's witnesses. That's right, questioning the other side's witnesses counts against your time. It's very important you prepare in advance so you don't end up wasting time arguing with them. The Court will often want to reserve time to issue a ruling, which is why in a three-hour hearing, you will have less than an hour and a half apiece.

Before you set your case for trial, you will want to try and figure out how much time you think you need to present all your evidence, so when the clerk asks you how much time you need for trial, you will know to double whatever time you come up with for yourself.

STARTING A TRIAL OUTLINE

A trial outline is your script. It lays out the points you want to make in your Opening Statement, your questions for each witness, the exhibits you will bring in through each witness, and the points you want to hit on in Closing Argument. The trial outline is there to remind you of everything that you need to bring out so you can be sure you present all your evidence in an organized manner. It helps you stay on track and manage your time. In my 10 years of practice, I have never gone to trial without a trial outline.

So far you have a trial *plan*. Now is where you start turning your trial plan into your trial outline. Here is a checklist of what you need to do to build a trial outline. Each item on this checklist is discussed in greater detail throughout this chapter, but this will provide you a snapshot of what you need to do. Use your trial plan as a checklist as you build your trial outline.

Steps to Building a Trial Outline

1. Make a list of all the evidence you want to present.

2. Beside each piece of evidence on that list, put the name or names of all witnesses who can authenticate that evidence.

3. Make your list of witnesses from that list.

4. If you have more than one witness who can authenticate a piece of evidence, select the best one to authenticate it.

5. List all the things you need each witness to tell the judge.

6. Organize this list into topics: (e.g.: Personal background, employment, observations of other parent and child, house, car, incomes).

7. Turn this list into questions.

8. Draft your closing argument.

9. Draft your opening statement.

Below are those same steps discussed in greater detail.

STEP 1: Make a list of all the evidence you want to present.

This evidence list will come directly from your trial plan. Evidence consists of testimony and hard proof, like documents. Testimony may not always be the most compelling form of evidence, but it is still evidence, and often the court will accept what a witness says as true if there is no reason to believe they are lying.

Go back to your trial plan and take a look at the facts you listed again.

- Make sure you have listed everything you need the judge to know.
- Refer to the law to ensure you have covered everything the judge will consider.

Once you've added everything you want the judge to know, ask yourself if you have any documents that will prove any facts you have listed. For example: report cards, bank statements, pay stubs, tax returns, police reports, diaries, emails, text messages, pictures, credit card bills. Make a list of all your evidence that you have to support what you want the judge to know about your case.

Step 2: Beside each piece of evidence on your list, put the names of all witnesses who can authenticate that evidence.

The first thing you need to know about witness testimony as you start this chapter is that anyone testifying is only allowed to testify as to their own observations. Witnesses cannot testify regarding anything someone else told them unless the person they are quoting happens to be the opposing party. Witnesses for either side can testify as to anything an opposing party said, or their own observations, but they cannot testify as to anything a third-party witness said.

How do you determine if you need to call any witnesses? You take a look at all the facts you listed in your trial plan. Who witnessed any of the events you described? Who was the only witness to any of the events you described? Did other people witness the stuff? Make a list of these people and what information they can provide. Don't forget to list yourself. You are a witness for your own case.

Evidence comes in through witnesses because witnesses have to verify the evidence's authenticity (meaning it has not been altered or falsified). For example, if you are introducing pictures, you usually need the person who was there or took the picture and can verify the picture has not been altered. In the alternative, if it is a picture you or someone downloaded off of your ex's Instagram, then the person who downloaded it needs to testify to verify the picture has not been altered from what was downloaded.

Documents may contain hearsay. For example, a police report contains hearsay. A report card contains hearsay. A medical chart record contains hearsay. You cannot bring just any document to court and have the court accept it as evidence. You need to have the person who can verify that it is accurate testify to authenticate it. There are many exceptions in the evidence rules which, if followed correctly, will allow you to introduce these documents into evidence successfully.

Here are some examples of documents you may bring and who you should have authenticate them.

Document	Who Must authenticate it
School records	School Records Custodian
Police report	Police Records Custodian
Medical chart	Records Custodian of Doctor's Office
Screen shot from phone	Person who received the texts/took the screen shot
Pictures	Photographer or someone in picture
Bank Statements	Records Custodian of Bank
Drug test results	Records Custodian from Testing Lab that Produced Document

If you want to bring in something like your child's medical chart or report card, you should just ask your ex if they will stipulate (agree on record in court) that it is authentic. Then you don't need to bring in anyone to authenticate it. I will discuss exactly how to have the witness authenticate evidence in Chapter 9.

There is a super cool rule that allows you to skip having the records custodian come to court. It's CRE 902, and says if you get a certified copy of the record, or submit a certificate of acknowledgment signed by the records custodian before a notary public, then the documents are self-authenticated and you do not need to haul that person into court. If you have to request records from a company, ask them if they can submit with it a Certificate of Self-Authentication. They will usually know what that means, and then when you introduce the document into evidence, you just need to cite the hearsay rule that applies to the document. The hearsay rules that you will usually need to use are outlined in Chapter 9.

Step 3: Make your list of witnesses from that list.

How many witnesses do you need? In domestic cases, parties tend to want to disclose 20 witnesses, even though there is probably only time for one or two. Parties tend to also want to bring in a bunch of "Character" witnesses to tell the judge what a good person they are, and what a piece of garbage the other party is. Don't waste time with this, please. The judge is not going to decide who to put your kids with because your mom and friends think your ex is a bad guy. This does not help you. It is more valuable to your case if you call a witness who can testify as to relevant observations, rather than character in general. Don't forget to include yourself.

Witnesses can only testify as to their observations. They cannot offer their opinion or testify regarding what YOU think of your ex. Testimony is evidence. It may not be the most compelling kind but it's something, and sometimes it is all you've got.

Some witnesses may require you subpoena them. Police officers require a subpoena. Other people may need it to get out of work. You can find instructions and the subpoena forms on the Court website, JDF forms 79, 80 and 80(a).

Step 4: If you have more than one witness who can authenticate a piece of evidence, select the best one.

Do not have three witnesses tell the same story. Judges get very impatient if you do this. Pick the best witness. Sure, you can have your other witnesses verify that they saw the same incident if they happen to be testifying for a different reason, but do not bring in three witnesses to tell one story.

Step 5: List all the things you need each witness to tell the judge.

Under each witness's name, list what they will be testifying to. This list is going to become your questions for them later. As you list these things, check them off of your trial plan. If you have anything left on your trial plan when you are done, go back to step one and figure out how you are going to bring that information in.

Step 6: Organize this list into topics: (e.g.: Personal background, employment, observations of other parent and child, house, car, incomes).

Under each witness name, organize your topics. Some witnesses may have very limited testimony, but you still need to present it in an organized fashion. A good way to do this is to put subheadings in your trial outline. Here is an example:

Background:
- Have witness testify as to how they know Mr. McFly and his kids

Incident
- Testify about observation at bar

Step 7: Turn this list into questions.

You can turn the above list into questions like this:

Background:
- How do you know Mr. McFly?
- How do you know his kids?

- Have you ever observed Mr. McFly with my kids?
- Incident
- Have you ever observed Mr. McFly with the kids at a bar?
- When?
- Where were you?
- What did you see them doing?
- How did you know that was them?
- How can you be sure Mr. McFly was drinking alcohol?
- Did this concern you? Why?

You want your questions to flow in a way that tells a story. When questioning your witness, it's helpful to the judge if you give "roadmaps" by saying to your witness, "now I'd like to discuss your employment. What do you do for a living…?" This makes it easy for your judge to understand where you are going and what topic you are on. The following section on How to Question Witnesses explains in greater detail how to draft witness questions.

Step 8: Draft your closing argument.

Your closing argument tells the judge how they should look at all the information you just presented and explains why the law supports what you are asking for. This will be covered in Chapter 10.

Step 9: Draft your opening statement.

This summarizes for the judge what the judge is about to hear and what you'll be asking the judge to order in the end. This will be covered in Chapter 10.

Here is an excerpt of a sample trial outline for your client, Sean Cash:

Opening Statement

- Ms. Cash ("Jane") filed a motion to relocate, averring several allegations against Mr. Cash consisting of neglect, mental abuse, and illegal acts of prostitution and drug use.
- Mr. Cash and his witnesses will testify today showing these are false, and only set forth to gain leverage in her case.
- Jane sought to relocate the child only after Mr. Cash filed a motion to modify child support based on the parenting time the parties were actually exercising.
- Mr. Cash requests the Court deny the relocation
- Mr. Cash requests the Court impute income to Jane of $3,767.17 gross monthly [$9/hour x 40 hours = 360 x 52 weeks/12 months = $1,560 per month. Add $2,207.17 average income in commissions = 3,767.17]

DIRECT OF S. CASH:

Jurisdiction:

- What is your name?
- Where do you live?
- Are you the Petitioner in this case?

Background

- What is your child's name?
- Were you married to the Respondent?

Employment

- What do you do for a living?
- How long have you done that?
- What do you earn currently?
- Who covers Chloe's health insurance? What is the cost of her portion?

Relocation Rebuttal

- How did Chloe handle her Mother moving to Tennessee (without saying what Chloe said)?
- Jane states she has maintained 50/50 custody since the divorce. What's your response?
- Jane states Chloe will have more family in Tennessee. What's your response? (bull)
- Jane states Chloe's Tennessee school is better than her Colorado school. What's your response?
- How is Chloe doing in school?
- Jane States you have engaged in drugs and prostitutes. What's your response?
- Jane states Chloe needs to be with her mother to help with feminine things. What's your response?
- Jane states you are not an active participant in Chloe's events. What's your response?
- Jane states she helps Chloe with homework on Skype every night. What's your response?
- Does Jane send Chloe cards? Gifts?
    - **Exhibit 4 (Card from Jane to Chloe)**
    - Do you recognize this? What is it? Accurate copy of original?
    - [enter into evidence]
    - What did Jane write to Chloe here?
    - What did you think of that?
    - Why does that concern you?

CROSS OF JANE CASH

Voluntarily underemployed

- Exhibit 6 (her sworn financial statement)
- You work 6 hours per week?
- At $9.00 per hour?
- Plus commissions?

    - o Exhibits 21, 22 and 23 – are these your pay stubs?
    - o You provided 11 pay stubs?
    - o From July 6 through October 6?
    - o Exhibit 21 You earned $74.95 year to date in commission as of July 14, 2022?
    - o Exhibit 22 You earned $1,465.47 year to date in commission as of October 6, 2022?

- Subtracting $74.95 from $1,465.47, you earned a total of $1,390.52 in commissions from July to October?
- Just working about 6 hours per week, according to your sworn financial statement.
- You have no children under 30 months of age?
- You are not mentally incapacitated?
- You are not physically incapacitated?
- You are not currently incarcerated and here on some kind of release?
- You are not in college at night?
- You are still pursuing an acting career?
- [$9/hour x 40 hours = 360 x 52 weeks/12 months = $1,560. + $2,207.17 average income in commissions = 3,767.17 gross monthly income.

Closing

[see chapter 10 for a comprehensive sample closing outline]

HOW TO QUESTION WITNESSES

Witnesses at trial tell their story by answering questions. When you question your own witnesses, this is called direct examination. The opposing party is given an opportunity to question the same witness about bad facts and inconsistencies. This is called cross examination. This section will instruct you on how to conduct both a direct and a cross examination.

You want to question your witnesses in a way that allows them to discuss observations through examples and stories. The more detailed, the more compelling the testimony will be. You do not want to have them testify using generalities. The best way to illustrate the difference is by a table:

Good Testimony (Observations)	Bad Testimony (Opinion/Character testimony/General)
He changes diapers, feeds the baby every night, reads them stories, and takes them out every Saturday so mom can have a break.	He's a good dad. Totally involved.
He has not baby-proofed the house. There are no plugs in the sockets, there are heavy, breakable objects within reach of a child, and he owns a vicious Rottweiler.	He is obviously a new dad. He has no clue what he's doing.
She called me a cocksucker, told me I'm a piece of trash and wished I would die a slow death, threatened to "cut me," threw a skillet at my head, and threw her coffee mug at me.	She is verbally and physically abusive.
I saw [opposing party] and heard her telling the kids their Father never pays his child support, doesn't care if they starve, and only visits them to keep his child support low- not because he wants to see them.	She's always alienating me from the kids.
The five times I went over to their house, I saw him flip off the neighbor, throw a chair, yell at the dog, kick in a wall, and each of those visits he yelled at the kids over little things like putting glasses in the dishwasher.	He's got an anger management problem.

Do you see how much stronger the first column is? This may seem obvious to some of you in looking at the table above, but I see this mistake made most often when *pro se* people and witnesses who were not properly prepared testify. People like to throw around phrases such as "verbally abusive" and "harassment." This is weak. Generalizations add absolutely no value to your case. They are just conclusory opinions based on nothing. Back up testimony with facts and observations and leave out the opinion.

DIRECT EXAMINATION

Direct examination consists of open-ended questions. Open ended questions begin with Who, What, When, Where, Why and How. The open-ended question is designed to let your witness speak more freely to tell a story. You are not allowed to ask closed-ended questions on direct because this is considered "leading" your witness. Leading the witness means you are asking a question in a way that suggests the answer. Some examples:

- Closed: You were born in New York City?
- Open: Where were you born?
- Closed: You came home at 10:00?
- Open: When did you get home?
- Closed: Did you meet Andy at the Cup o' Joe on Main?
- Open: Who did you see at Cup o' Joe?

When preparing your witnesses for direct, you will want to go over your questions with them in advance, so they know what you are going to be asking them. You do not want to be surprised by any of your own witnesses' answers at trial. Make sure you draft your questions so you can draw specific examples from your witnesses where necessary. Tell your witnesses to only answer the question asked by the questioner while on the stand. Do not ask your witness to lie. However, you may coach them to help them tell a more concise story.

When you meet with your witness before trial, prepare them using this checklist:

» Tell your witness to tell the truth, even if they think it makes you look bad. [If you are afraid of something your witness might say, either on direct or cross, then don't call that witness.]

- Only answer the question asked. Do not offer any additional information other than what was asked. If you are asked "when", give a timeframe. If you are asked "who", give a name; etc. If you are asked a yes/no question, give a yes/no answer. Assure them that you will have a chance to ask you more questions on redirect if something comes out on cross that seems negative.
- Tell them, "be as nice to the cross examiner as you are to me. It will add credibility to your testimony." Witnesses who are friendly on direct and nasty on cross lose credibility and look like they have something to hide.
- Dress appropriately for court.
- Be respectful to the court and questioners.

CROSS EXAMINATION

Cross examination consists of closed-ended questions. A closed-ended question suggests the answer and is a "Yes/No" type of question. These questions typically can begin with "Isn't it true..." or end with "right?" For example, "isn't it true you were home on Saturday?" or "You were home on Saturday, right?" Often, the cross-examiner will remove both that beginning and end, and use voice inflection at the end of the statement making it a question: "You were home on Saturday?"

When you are cross examining, stick to closed-ended questions. An open-ended question to an adverse witness does nothing to help you, but helps that witness explain away bad facts. This is a very difficult thing for people to get away from. Parties often are tempted to cross examine the same way they argue- by asking rhetorical, snotty questions based on emotion. Do not do this. On cross, don't ask why. Stay away from the question you don't already know the answer to.

In preparing your cross, use your "facts beyond dispute" because these are facts the other party cannot possibly dispute that help you.

Bad Cross (Arguing with Witness)	Good Cross (Stick with Facts Beyond Dispute)
You asked me for my bank statement months ago, but you didn't get me yours until three days before trial.	You asked me for my bank statement months ago? On October 9th? And I sent it to you October 10th? And I asked you for yours on October 10th? You didn't send it to me in October? Or in November? Or in December? In fact, you sent it to me three days before trial?
Why would she want to live with you? You just watch TV all day. (*Witness will argue back on this one)*	Isn't it true on Sundays you watch the 11:15 Football game? Then the 2:15? The pregame show? Post-game shows? NFL Prime Time?
Don't you agree you have a drug problem? (*Witness will split hairs with you on this one*)	You started using pot at 16? You were arrested on drug charges at 18? You have used meth? Twice? You had a dilute drug test in 2015? You relapsed on meth in 2016? You were drunk when you were arrested in 2018? You blame the crime on you having been too drunk to know what you were doing?
You just don't want to work so I'll have to pay for you, isn't that right?	You've been a realtor since 2012? You sold 5 houses in 2013? 6 in the 2014? 7 in the 2015? Then 1 in 2016? 2 in 2017? 1 in 2018? You haven't tried direct mail marketing? You don't do door knockers? You don't keep a formal client database. You don't cold call. You don't email people for follow up anymore. You don't hold open houses anymore (since 2017). Even though you got 2-3 leads off of those? You stated you only get "nosey neighbors" coming in? You haven't called other agents to offer to hold their house open since about 2014? You haven't taken gifts to clients since 2017. You only attend 3-4 trainings a year. Trainings are offered every month. Your last one was Summer 2018. You don't set aside any specific amount of commissions for marketing.

HOW TO QUESTION EXPERTS

If you have an expert testifying for you in court, you must first have the expert explain to the Court what makes them an expert. This is called laying foundation, and you do this through questions of your witness at the beginning. Then you must ask the court to recognize this person as an expert in that particular field. To lay foundation, you will start your questioning of the witness by asking about their educational and professional background. When you are done, the other side has an opportunity to "voir dire" the witness, which really just means cross examining on the questions you just asked. Then the judge will decide whether to qualify that person as an expert. It helps to introduce the expert's resume (also called a curriculum vitae, or "CV" in legal world) into evidence.

Here is a sample of how qualifying an expert may look:

- Please state your name.
- What do you do for a living?
- Are you licensed as a realtor? When did you get licensed?
- How long have you been doing that?
- What does the job entail?
- Do you market to get clients?
- How much revenue have you earned the past three years as a realtor?
- Have you given any lectures in this field of real estate marketing and sales? How many?
- Have you received any honors or awards in this field?
- Do you have resume? (admit resume into evidence)
- Did you prepare a report in this case?
- What materials did you review in creating your report?
- Do you believe that your testimony will be helpful in assisting the judge understand real estate marketing and sales?

Your honor, at this time I tender this witness as an expert in the field of Real Estate Sales and Marketing.

Voir dire (challenging the expert qualification) may look very similar to the qualification of the expert. That is why during the questioning, you need to listen for what *wasn't* asked. For example:

- Do you run your own business?
- Have you ever run your own business?
- Have you only sold residential real estate?
- Have you only sold residential in the metro area?
- Have you taught any courses on real estate marketing and sales?
- Have you published anything on the subject of real estate marketing and sales?
- Have you tried every marketing strategy you listed?
- Have you ever been qualified as an expert before?

Your honor – I object to this witness being qualified as an expert in this field because he has not ….

I recommend drafting your entire script for how to intend to qualify your expert in your trial outline to ensure you stay on track. If the other side has an expert, review that expert's credentials before trial and prepare your voir dire in advance on how you can try to attack their credentials.

WHAT TO BRING TO COURT

Now that you have selected your evidence and witnesses, what do you do?

When you enter something into evidence, you will never get it back. You cannot get a text message into evidence by showing your actual phone to the judge. You need to bring the screen shot, printed as an exhibit, and include the entire conversation. If you showed the actual phone to the judge, you'd lose the phone.

Also, if you are including emails and screen shots of conversations as exhibits, you must bring the entire conversation. This is called the rule of completeness. The other side may object if you try and enter only a portion of a conversation into evidence, and the court will reject it. You must print the whole conversation.

You must bring four copies of everything you want the Court to consider: a copy for yourself, a copy for the opposing party, a copy for the witness on the stand, and a copy for the judge. If you bring only one copy, the judge will often refuse to look at it. Select your exhibits, label them, and make four exhibit notebooks to bring to Court. When labeling, the Petitioner is numbered exhibits (1, 2, 3) and the Respondent is lettered exhibits (A, B, C).

You will need to bring the witnesses who can authenticate each specific document if you cannot authenticate it yourself. For example, for report cards, you may need to have a school records custodian come testify as to its authenticity. Police reports may need to be authenticated by a police officer or records custodian. You will have disclosed your witnesses 63 days in advance, but you may want to remind them that you need them there the day of trial, and what time you will need them.

Most importantly, don't forget to print and bring your trial outline! Your outline should cover your opening statement, questions for each witness, and your closing argument. The more prepared you are in advance, the better trial is likely to go. You do not want to show up and wing it.

- Four exhibit notebooks (which include table of contents of exhibits)
- Legal authority you are relying on
- Trial outline (open, direct examination, cross examination, closing argument)
- Notepad to take notes
- Two pens

After years of practicing, I failed to bring the exhibit notebooks for the witness and judge to the hearing. Fortunately, I had a very professional attorney on the other side of the case who was gracious enough to work with me. Attorney in Englewood, CO.

CHAPTER 9: PRESENTING EVIDENCE

I discussed in the previous chapter that evidence comes in through witnesses. When you introduce evidence to the judge, you need to have a witness authenticate it. You don't just bring a pile of papers to court and hand them to a judge. This chapter will explain *how* you authenticate the evidence to get the Court to consider it, how to object, and basic evidence rules.

HOW TO GET THE DOCUMENT INTO EVIDENCE

Getting a document "into evidence" means getting the court to agree to consider the document.

When introducing a document into evidence, whether through yourself or through a witness, you must lay foundation. Laying foundation refers to the process of having the person who is authenticating the document verify why they know it is authentic. Generally, laying foundation consists of three questions:

1. Do you recognize this?
2. What is it?
3. Is this an accurate representation of the original?

These three questions assume you already covered who this person is and why they are the person with the personal knowledge of the document. If you have not covered this, you need to. For example, if this person is going to be verifying a business record, and the person is the records custodian at that business, that may look like this:

1. State your name
2. Where do you work?
3. What is your job there?
4. What are your job duties?
5. Based on that, do you have personal knowledge of the contents of the Smith file?
6. How do you have that personal knowledge?
7. When is the last time you reviewed the Smith file?
8. Would you recognize it today if you saw it?

Once the person has answered these questions verifying they recognize it, it's accurate, and telling the court generally what the document is, you can ask the court to enter it into evidence. When laying this foundation, the witness cannot testify as to the content of the document when answering the question, "what is it?" They must simply give a general description of the document, such as "It's a bank statement" or "it's an email from Andy."

When you ask, "do you recognize this?", if your witness answers no, then you cannot introduce it through that witness. If they answer "yes," then you can move on to the next question.

Depending on what the document is, the court may require you to "lay more foundation." This means the court wants to hear more about why this witness is the person who can authenticate it. An example of laying more foundation may be:

1. Who took this picture?
2. Who is in the picture?
3. Whose phone was this screen shot taken from?
4. When was the picture taken?
5. How do you know when it was taken?
6. Who received the email?

7. Who printed the email?

Here is an example of introducing a screen shot of text messages into evidence.

Q: Do you recognize this?
  A: Yes
Q: What is it?
  A: Screen shots of texts between me and Andy
Q: Is this an accurate representation of the original?
  A: Yes
Q: Who typed what is in blue?
  A: Me
Q: Who typed what is in yellow?
  A: Andy
Q: How do you know that was Andy?
  A: Because his number is saved in my phone and we have texted before.
Q: When did this conversation take place?
  A: January 11, 2018
Q: How do you know that?
  A: It is date stamped on page 1.
Q: Is this the entire conversation concerning this subject matter?
  A: Yes
Q: From whose phone were these screen shots taken?
  A: Mine
Q: Did you take them?
  A: Yes

Your Honor, at this time I move to enter Exhibit A into evidence.

Here is an example of introducing a business record, such as a report card from a school.

Q: State your name

A: Chadley Cooper

Q: Where do you work?

A: Gaga Elementary School

Q: What is your job there?

A: Records Custodian

Q: What are your job duties?

A: Filing, maintaining records, light clerical work

Q: Based on that, do you have personal knowledge of the contents of the Lawrence file?

A: Yes

Q: How do you have that personal knowledge?

A: Because I have maintained that record and seen it at work.

Q: When is the last time you reviewed the Lawrence file?

A: In preparation for this case.

Q: Would you recognize it today if you saw it?

A: Yes

Q: Do you recognize this?

A: Yes

Q: What is it?

A: Jessica Lawrence's report card.

Q: Is this an accurate representation of the original?

A: Yes

Q: Is this a record that is kept in the course of regularly conducted business by the school?

A: Yes

Q: Is it the regular practice of the school to create these records?

A: Yes.

Your Honor, at this time I move to enter Exhibit A into evidence.

Once you get your documents together, you may want to sit down with an attorney and discuss how to properly authenticate your specific exhibits. In law school, there is an entire year devoted to evidence - learning objections and how to properly authenticate. This can be complicated and you want to ensure you get it right. The SRLOCs (discussed in the Appendix) and attorneys in legal aid clinics, and those who offer unbundled services, can provide you with tailored assistance for your specific evidence.

HOW TO OBJECT

You may need to object to improper questions the other side asks your witness in order to protect yourself. For example, if a witness is asked what your children's teacher told her, this is hearsay and it should not be allowed in. So, you'll need to stand up and say, "Objection, Hearsay" with the confidence and gusto of someone who completed three years of law school! This section will explain how to do that.

Oftentimes on TV shows lawyers simply yell "Objection!" and the court automatically responds "sustained" or "overruled." Must be nice. In real life, you must have a valid legal reason to object. Your objection must be based on one of the rules of evidence which govern what information is and is not allowed to come in at trial.

The way you object is you state "objection" followed by your evidentiary reason: "Objection, hearsay;" "Objection, relevance;" "Objection, lack of foundation;" Therefore, you need to know some basic evidence rules so you'll know what to object to.

Knowing these rules is important to preparing your trial for a few reasons:

1. If you can anticipate which of your questions may be objectionable, you can try rewording them or preparing the right evidence to overcome the objection.
2. You can plan your objections in advance many times by simply reviewing the other side's pre-disclosed exhibits.

Sometimes the information you want to get in at trial is not objectionable but the way you ask your witness about it *is* objectionable. You need to know some basic evidence rules to draft your questions.

BASIC EVIDENCE RULES

The Colorado Rules of Evidence (CRE) are available to the public. These rules govern what is and is not admissible, as well as how evidence may be presented. To access the Rules, Google "Lexis Advance Colorado Legal Resources" and you will see a link to Colorado Legal Resources – Lexis. Click on that and you will be taken to a page where you can access Colorado statutes, Colorado Constitution, and court rules. Click on "Local, State, and Federal Court Rules" and then scroll down to the Colorado Rules of Evidence.

Here are some common rules of evidence you may need to know for trial.

Hearsay. CRE 803.

What to say. "Objection! Hearsay!"

Definition: An out of court statement offered for its truth.

In Plain English: The witness is quoting something someone said at some point before the trial and offering that quote as proof of something.

Example: "Andy said the light was red." (Offered to prove the light was red); "My kids tell me they never want to go to their mom's" (offered to prove the kids never want to go to their mom's).

Reason this is not allowed in: There's no way to verify its accuracy.

Exceptions to the Hearsay Rule. There are certain exceptions that allow hearsay into evidence if the proper foundation is laid and the right person authenticates it. Some of these rules that you may find helpful are:

- Verbal acts: the words are the act. Conspiracy, contract, bribery, offer, acceptance, defamation, cancellation, misrepresentation, permission.
- Effect on listener: reason listener acted the way he did.
- Prior inconsistent statements, under oath at a prior proceeding.
- Admission by party opponent.
- Statement against interest
- Dying declaration.
- Statement of state of mind at issue (insanity, e.g.: declaring, "I am the Pope")
- Excited utterance (Must be startling event, made under stress of excitement, concerning the event)
- Present sense impression (Declarant statement as he's per-

ceiving the event)

- Statements to doctors for purpose of diagnosis or treatment.
- Public records
- Business Records (Made at or near time, by person with knowledge, kept in regular course of business – unless source or circumstances indicate lack of trustworthiness.
- A complete list of the hearsay rules and exceptions are in CRE 803 through 807.

Hearsay exceptions that may apply to documents you are generally trying to get in are as follows:

Business Records and Medical Records	CRE 803(6)
Public records, like police reports	CRE 803(8)
Market reports	CRE 803(17)
Vital statistics	CRE 803(9)
Real Property Interest	CRE 803(14)

Relevance. CRE 402, 403.

What to say. "Objection! Relevance!"

Definition: Information is irrelevant or it is relevant but its value is outweighed by unfair prejudice to your case.

In Plain English: the information has little or nothing to do with your case, OR it is mildly relevant but it will unfairly make the judge dislike the other side for irrelevant reasons.

Example: Your ex wants to testify regarding your affairs during the marriage, and your unusual sexual preferences.

Reason this is not allowed in: It is a waste of the court's time because it will not help the judge to make a decision; it will unfairly turn the judge against you on an issue that the judge is not supposed to base the decision on.

Examples of things that ARE logically relevant and may be admissible even if it involves another time, event or person not involved in the case.

- Causation: like showing other people got sick at same restaurant, same day
- Prior Accidents: other people have hit the same bridge – shows notice.
- Intent/State of mind: showing employer's history of discrimination
- Rebuttal: showing it's not impossible for mouse to get in Coke-it happened before.
- Comparable sales to establish value of something.
- Habit: E.g.: he always runs red lights.

Testimony is irrelevant if the probative value is substantially outweighed by danger of:

- Unfair prejudice
- Confusion of issues
- Misleading jury
- Undue delay
- Waste of time
- Cumulative evidence

Lack of Foundation; Speculative. CRE 602.

What to say. "Objection! Calls for Speculation!" OR "Lack of Foundation!"

Definition: Testimony that is not based on the witness's personal knowledge.

In Plain English: The witness may only testify to matters that he has personal knowledge of. He cannot guess.

Example of speculative: Question is asked, "what do you think the effects are on the children of your wife introducing the kids to the new guy so soon?"

Reason this is not allowed in: It is opinion that does not add value to the judge's decision.

Example of lack of foundation: Question is asked, "What drugs has your ex used in his life?"

Reason this is not allowed in: Its accuracy cannot be verified.

How to lay foundation: First ask, "do you have knowledge of the drugs your ex has used in the past? What is that knowledge based on?" You basically need the witness to verify the knowledge is based on either her own observations or on what the other party told her.

Privilege. CRE 501, 502.

What to say. "Objection! Privileged!"

Definition: Testimony that is private as between attorney and client, doctor/therapist and client, or priest and parishioner.

In Plain English: Your conversations with an attorney, doctor, therapist, and priest are private and you do not have to testify to that information.

Example: Question is asked, "did your attorney discuss this with you?"

Reason this is not allowed in: Public policy is that you should have faith that your conversations with these entities are protected so that you will be able to fully disclose your case or medical needs and get the help you need without worry that these conversations will be used against you one day.

Settlement negotiations. CRE 408.

What to say. "Objection! Protected Settlement Negotiation!"

Definition: Settlement negotiations are confidential and cannot be disclosed at trial.

In Plain English: Your offers to settle are private, and neither party may disclose what happens in settlement negotiations, whether or not they occurred in mediation.

Example: Party tries to testify, "well at mediation, you were willing to . . .."

Reason this is not allowed in: Public policy is that you should have faith that your offers to compromise will not be used against you. Otherwise, people will be afraid to negotiate at all and settlement will be less likely.

- It is important to remember that the above list is not a complete list of all the rules of evidence. You may want to review the rules of evidence more on your own or consult with an attorney regarding your specific case.

Also remember that even if you make a perfectly valid and legal objection, the Court may overrule it. Any attorney will tell you, judges sometimes overrule valid objections and sustain terrible ones for no apparent reason. Literally hundreds of appeals are filed every year simply because attorneys believe a judge made a wrong evidentiary ruling.

CHAPTER 10: OPENING STATEMENTS AND CLOSING ARGUMENTS

There is a reason we call these Opening *Statement* and Closing *Argument*. The opening statement is a summary of the facts. In the opening, you are going to just tell the judge what you want and what you intend to offer to prove it. By contrast, in the closing argument, you are going to tie the case together in a neat little bow for the judge, summarizing the evidence that came in and explaining how, under the law, you win with the facts that were presented.

For example, an opening statement may look like this:

> *Your Honor, today I am asking the Court to grant my request to relocate the children to Houston. The Court will hear the children spent the first 9 and 11 years of their lives there, respectively; they have grandparents on both their mother and father's side there; they have many friends; and they will return to the same school their friends attend.*

In an opening statement, you should be able to start your sentences with "the evidence will show . . . ." If you can start your sentence with that, it is not argument.

Do not give a long opening statement. This is a roadmap for the judge - nothing else. You do not want to eat up your time in a lengthy opening. Often, judges will ask parties if they want to waive opening. This is because the judge will consider your Trial Management Certificate (discussed in Chapter 11) to be your opening statement. If you are offered this, it is advisable to accept the offer to waive.

The closing argument is your chance to tell the judge how they should tie all the information together under the law, the way you see it. The closing should be professional and matter of fact. This is not the time to try and mimic what you have seen on TV, with a loud monologue and big hand gestures. Instead, remind the judge what the legal standard is, and the evidence that was presented that supports your position.

One particular tactic I like to use is to tell the court what it *didn't* hear. For example, if the standard for modification is "best interest of the child," and the opposing party never mentioned this but instead talked all about Father's rights (which is NOT a factor in determining custody), I would point out to the court that the other side made it all about them and presented NO evidence on how the requested modification serves the best interests of the child.

To come up with your closing argument, use the IRAC format I discussed in Chapter 1, Litigation section. State the issue briefly, start with the law that governs what it is you are requesting, and format your close based on that. Tie in the evidence presented under each legal burden you must prove, because this is how the Court will evaluate the case. The Court will start with the law and determine whether the parties met their burdens. If you are unsure what yours or the other party's burdens of proof are, consult with an attorney in a legal aid clinic.

The format you should follow is this:

1. State the **Issue** before the court. If there are more than one, take one at a time:

2. Cite the **Rule** of Law.
3. **Apply** the law to the evidence that was presented in trial.
4. **Conclusion**. Summarize why you win.

Here is a sample of a closing argument:

[ISSUE] *We are here on an allocation of parental rights and responsibilities.* **[RULE]** *The Court must determine what is in the best interest of the child under § 14-10-124, C.R.S.*

[APPLICATION] *The Court heard today that I am requesting majority parenting time with Mr. Blaine having Rick and Elsa every other weekend. Mr. Blaine disagrees and wants more time with the kids. Rick is only 8 so he is not sufficiently mature to express a preference however Elsa is 16 years old. The CFI testified that Elsa wishes to live with me the majority of the time and the CFI believes she is mature enough to have expressed a reasoned opinion.*

The Court heard that Rick and Elsa have been in my primary care since they were babies. Specifically, I was the one who fed them, bathed them, and took them to all their medical appointments. I am the one who cuddles and plays with them more in the evenings and helps with homework. I am the one who got Elsa enrolled in therapy after the volleyball incident, which Mr. Blaine objected to.

The Court also heard testimony that I live in the school district where the kids are enrolled, while Mr. Blaine has moved into an apartment downtown. It would be a hardship on the children to commute to school from his home during the week because they would have to wake up about 30 minutes earlier. Although Mr. Blaine works from home and has flexibility to pick the kids up from school that I do not have, I have arranged for a neighbor who has children in the same school as Rick to walk him home with their own child, and Elsa will be getting her own car so she can drive herself.

The court heard testimony of my bipolar disorder, and I explained to the Court that I have not had any issues and have been controlling it successfully with medication since 2014. This is not an issue the Court needs to be concerned about and was brought up by Mr. Blaine as a red herring to make me look mentally unstable.

Regarding the ability of each party to encourage the sharing of love, the court heard testimony that Mr. Blaine has been heard disparaging me to the children when he called me a "bad mom" and said I blow money. This is not in the best interests of the children to hear. I will never disparage Mr. Blaine to the children.

The Court heard that my mother and sister live within 10 miles of me and see the children every week at least one time. Mr. Blaine's family lives in Missouri and visits maybe one time per year. The children are very bonded to my side of the family, including their four cousins.

I believe both Mr. Blaine and I have the ability to place the children's needs ahead of our own needs. However Mr. Blaine has failed to do so at every opportunity, with disparaging me to the children, getting babysitters on the days he has had the children so he can go to bars, and refusing to enroll Elsa in advanced Cheer because it took place during football on Sunday. In addition, Mr. Blaine moved out of the marital home while I was out of town with the kids, with no explanation to them in advance, which was deeply harmful emo-

tionally to them.

The Court heard also about my DUI. However, the Court also heard the children were not in the car, I completed the terms of my probation, including alcohol education and monitored sobriety, and there have been no incidents since that date.

[CONCLUSION] *Based on all of this, I believe it is in the best interests of the children to reside primarily with me and to live with Mr. Blaine every other weekend from Friday after school until Sunday at 4pm. I am asking for joint decision making. I have submitted a proposed parenting plan outlining the details of this plan and have a courtesy copy for the court in the exhibit notebook as exhibit 10.*

In the sample closing argument, the party outlines for the Court the facts of the case in the same order as the best interest of the child factors listed in § 14-10-124, C.R.S. This is helpful for the judge who is vigorously taking notes. She summarizes neatly into a concise package what the Court needs to focus on and eliminates irrelevant evidence that may have been brought out in trial. It is not angry-sounding and does not contain any rhetoric or inflammatory language.

Remember – maintaining professionalism adds to your own credibility with the court.

CHAPTER 11: FINAL FORMS

Whether you resolved your case at mediation, or you are about to go to a final hearing to finalize your case, you must prepare certain final documents for your case.

The forms you need to submit depend on whether you settled or not, and whether your case is pre-decree or post-decree. This chapter is organized by the forms, followed by a list of the types of cases in which it would be needed, so you can look through and quickly determine whether you need a particular form. I have also included a brief description of issues you may want to consider when completing these forms to prevent future problems or disputes from arising.

The final forms you usually must prepare are:

- Trial Management Certificate (if you are going to trial)
- Parenting Plan (if there are children), JDF 1113
- Separation Agreement (if this is a divorce, legal separation or annulment), JDF 1115
- Affidavit for Decree without Appearance (if you qualify), JDF 1201.
- Proposed Decree (if divorce, legal separation, or annulment), JDF 1116
- Proposed Support Order (if there are children and/or spousal support), JDF 1117

If you settled your case, your mediator may have prepared most of these forms for you. If not, you need to complete these to submit to the Court.

If you have not settled your case, you should submit a proposed parenting plan and separation agreement that outline what you are asking the Court to order. This just helps the judge compartmentalize your requests and helps you to think of everything you needed to think of.

TRIAL MANAGEMENT CERTIFICATE

This is submitted in both pre- and post-decree cases of all types. There is not a JDF form for this, so you have to create it yourself.

If you are going to trial, the Court requires you submit a Trial Management Certificate, or TMC. The TMC tells the Court what the issues are in the case and what each side's position is.

C.R.C.P. 16.2(h) requires the parties to submit a Trial Management Certificate and exchange exhibits with each other seven days before trial. Ideally, the court prefers to get a Joint Trial Management Certificate ("JTMC"). However, if you cannot get the opposing party to work with you to put one together, you should still submit your own TMC.

The TMC must state stipulations, undisputed facts, requests for attorney fees, disputed issues, specific points of law you are relying on, lists of your witnesses, and list of exhibits. The list of exhibits must include a pretty recently updated sworn financial statement.

Here is a sample excerpt from a JTMC:

[CAPTION]

JOINT TRIAL MANAGEMENT CERTIFICATE

COME NOW the parties, Petitioner, Sue Ellen Duffy, and Respondent, J.R. Duffy, and hereby submit their Joint Trial Management Certificate.

I. <u>CERTIFICATE OF COMPLIANCE:</u>

Petitioner and Respondent certify they have worked collaboratively to complete this JTMC.

II. <u>NATURE OF THE HEARING:</u>

This action is set for a half-day hearing on January 20, 2024, on the following motions:

A. Petitioner's Motion to Modify Allocation of Parental Responsibilities.

B. Petitioner's Motion to Modify Decision Making.

III. <u>PRETRIAL MOTIONS:</u>

A. None pending.

IV. <u>STIPULATIONS AND UNDISPUTED FACTS:</u>

A. The parties were married on July 31, 2014 and separated February 21, 2019.

B. The parties were divorced July 7, 2019.

C. The parties are the biological parents of one child: James Richard Duffy born October 29, 2015.

D. The current Parenting Plan in place was ordered on July 7, 2019. This Parenting Plan provided a parenting schedule. A copy of the Parenting Plan is attached hereto as Exhibit 1.

E. At present, Petitioner has majority parenting time at 209 days of the year, and Respondent has the child 156 days.

F. A Child and Family Investigator, Linda Ewing, was appointed in this matter, and his report was filed on December 22, 2023.

V. <u>DISPUTED ISSUES:</u>

A. Parenting Time:

a. Petitioner's position:

b. Respondent's position:

B. Decision Making:

a. Petitioner's position:

b. Respondent's position:

Each party will fill out their own position in this section.

VI. SPECIFIC POINTS OF LAW:

A. Petitioner will rely on the following points of law:

B. Respondent may rely on the following points of law:

VII. LAY WITNESSES:

A. Petitioner's lay witnesses are:

B. Respondent's lay witnesses are:

VIII. EXPERT WITNESSES

A. Petitioner's expert witnesses are:

B. Respondent's expert witnesses are:

IX. EXHIBITS

A. List of the Petitioner's exhibits:

B. List of the Respondent's exhibits:

Each party will fill out their own witnesses and exhibits in a JTMC.

VII. FINANCIAL AFFIDAVITS:

A. Petitioner filed an updated Sworn Financial Statement on December 7, 2023.

B. Respondent filed an updated Sworn Financial Disclosure on December 13, 2023.

XI. ALTERNATE DISPUTE RESOLUTION:

The parties participated in mediation on November 28, 2023 at 9:30 a.m. with Pamela Barnes. The parties were unable to resolve any of the disputed issues.

Sue Ellen Duffy Petitioner	J.R. Duffy Respondent

When working with the opposing party on completing a JTMC, I recommend initiating the drafting at least a week before it needs to be submitted to the Court. I advise asking the other party to have it back to you with their additions a day or two in advance of the due date. Do not alter anything the opposing party wrote., no matter what they write. Instead, use your own section to counter anything you do not agree with in their section.

PARENTING PLAN

This is submitted in both pre- and post-decree cases involving custody.

The parenting plan is JDF 1113. This is the document that will become a court order that you and the other parent will rely on concerning parenting days, exchange times, holidays, decisions, extracurricular activities, and so on. The more specific you can be on every aspect of it, the less likely you will be to have future disputes concerning interpretation. Instead of just stating you get Thanksgiving and he gets Christmas in even years, list the exchange days and times.

Often, parents who go through an amicable divorce leave the parenting plan vague, because they assume since the divorce was amicable, they will be able to agree on vague terms in the future. This may be true, but this is risky, because if that fails and you do end up arguing, you have no recourse to resolve the dispute. Be specific now, and you can prevent this from happening.

Some parents put in an agreement that they intend to be flexible with each other, and the parenting plan is merely a backup in the event of a disagreement. Honestly, this goes without saying, but if it makes you and the other parent feel better to put it in, go ahead.

Add a Non-Disparagement Clause

You may also want to add a non-disparagement clause. This is a clause that says both parents agree not to disparage the other parent in the presence of the children or to encourage other people to do so. This just helps to remind both parents that no matter what happens and how angry you get, you are under a court order not to disparage the other parent.

Add a Mediation Requirement

Adding a mediation requirement helps tempers cool, prevents hasty filings against the other parent, and helps the parties to focus on settlement in future disputes. A mediation requirement may look something like this:

> *In the event of future disputes, prior to filing any motions (except for emergency motions or motions to modify child support), the parties agree to participate, in good faith, in mediation in an attempt to resolve the dispute. If one party refuses to participate in mediation or to schedule a two-hour minimum mediation within a reasonable amount of time, the other party will be deemed to have complied with this requirement.*

The reason for the child support exception in the above example is because child support is modifiable back to the date of filing the motion. So, it is important that a party file the motion sooner in order to preserve that retroactive date.

Define How You are Dividing Extracurricular Activity Expenses

There is not a section on the Court form directing parents to do this, but this is a dispute that comes up often. Who is going to pay for extracurriculars for the kids? What If the other parent enrolls them without talking to you first? What if it is insanely expensive?

In one case, the parenting plan required the parents to split extracurricular activities in proportion to their respective incomes, which required mom to pay 10% and dad to pay 90%. Mom then enrolled the two boys into several football camps and clubs without dad's consent, costing $6,000 per year total. She then sent the bill to dad and threatened contempt if he did not cover 90%.

I do not have a recommendation for you on how to divide this. But I can give you some things to consider:

- Do you want to divide these *pro rata* (in proportion to your incomes) or 50/50?
- Do you want to state that you both have to agree to the activity in order to seek contribution from the other parent?
- Do you want to agree that you will only enroll the kids in activities during your own days? (This may be tough, depending on your parenting time schedule).
- Do you have to agree that you each get to enroll the kid in one activity, not to exceed a certain cost, and demand contribution from the other parent?

You might want to add in that this can be modified in the future based on changes in child support modification. That way, you are preserving your right to change it and preserving the court's jurisdiction to modify it as part of child support.

Define Phone/Skype Calls

These days, most kids have their own phone, making this probably a moot point. But for those parents who have young children, you may want to add in a clause that says you get to talk to you child certain days and times when they are in the other parent's care. It can be hard for children to be away from one parent for a long period of time. This allows the child to have more continuity of contact with both parents despite living in two homes.

SEPARATION AGREEMENT

This form is submitted in only pre-decree divorce or legal separation cases.

- The Separation Agreement is JDF 1115. This is the agreement parties enter into to divide all their assets and debts and governs any spousal support payments in their divorce or legal separation.

Set Reasonable Deadlines for Everything

If you don't set a deadline to act, it is unenforceable. You cannot complain to the Court that your ex is in contempt because he failed to transfer title to the car, or refinance the house, or deliver paperwork to you, if the sky is the limit on when he is allowed to do that.

A reasonable deadline gives the person enough time to complete the task but ensures you both can move on in a reasonable amount of time. For example, it may take 90 days to complete a home refinance. However, it only takes about 30 days to complete title transfer and delivery of that title on the car. Make sure you give enough time without getting taken advantage of. As a general rule, I try and wrap things up within 30 days and require refinance within 90.

Don't Quitclaim a Property Until You're Off the Loan

Ownership in the marital home is your insurance that the other party will remove you from the loan. It is absolutely crucial you remain on title until you get proof that the ex has refinanced the property into her own name, removing you from the loan. Only then should you deliver the Quit Claim deed. State that this is a condition in the Separation Agreement. Here is some sample language.

> *The parties own real property known as 123 Oak Street, Denver, CO 80126. The Husband hereby agrees to convey the Wife any interest he may have in said property by Quitclaim deed, which shall be held by the escrow agent, which may deliver the Quitclaim deed to the Wife only after the Wife refinances the property into her own name. The Wife shall remain solely liable for any debts, obligations, taxes, liens, encumbrances, or any other liabilities or obligations which have arisen or may arise in the future concerning said property and shall indemnify and hold the Husband harmless therefrom.*

If an attorney drafted the Separation Agreement, you may find a lot of standard contract language within the document that you do not understand. Here are some standard contract provisions you may run into and what they mean.

» BANKRUPTCY WAIVER. Typically, this provision will state that your child support or maintenance obligation are not dischargeable in bankruptcy. This is already law and this provision is typically included to simply advise the parties that this is already the law.

- HEALTH, ACCIDENT, AUTO AND LIFE INSURANCE. You may see this provision which should state that both parties agree that each one is free to maintain their own insurance, the other person claiming they should be a beneficiary.
- DOCUMENTS AND INSTRUMENTS. This provision may be at the end as a catch all to state that, if it is not clear by the agreement, the parties will execute any documents necessary to carry out the terms of the agreement.
- DISCLOSURE AND DISCOVERY. This provision will have both parties certifying that the provided full disclosure of their assets and liabilities, that they relied on each other 's disclosures, and if they find out the other person lied, they have the right to reopen the case.
- MODIFICATION. This provision states that the Separation Agreement constitutes the entire agreement between the parties and that you cannot rely on any promises that were made that were not put into the Agreement. This is an important one because this means if you believe you have an agreement with the other side but it was not put into the Separation Agreement, DO NOT SIGN THE SEPARATION AGREEMENT until you get that put in.
- MUTUAL RELEASE. This provision says the Separation Agreement resolves all of the issues between you and the ex, and so you are "releasing" the ex from any claims you previously had, either because they are resolved in the Separation Agreement or you let them go.
- WAIVER OF CLAIMS TO ESTATES. This says you are waiving your right to inherit from your ex.
- GOVERNING LAW. This provision typically states that if a dispute arises later concerning anything in the Separation Agreement, the dispute will be resolved by applying the laws of

whatever State is stated in this provision (even if you transfer jurisdiction to another State), which since you're reading this book probably will say "Colorado."

- DECREE AND COURT ORDER. This states that both parties intend for the Separation Agreement to become a Court Order and want the Court to enter a Decree of Dissolution of Marriage or Legal Separation.
- COURT CLERK AS COMMISSIONER. This is a pretty cool clause. This says that if your ex does not end up signing what they are supposed to sign in order to transfer title to something like real estate, the Clerk of Court can sign the document in their place to complete the transfer. This prevents difficult exes from being hold-outs.
- TIME LIMITS. This is a catch-all provision that puts a time limit to act under the Separation Agreement if it is not otherwise stated.
- SEVERABILITY. This says that if any part of the Separation Agreement turns out to be invalid or unenforceable, the rest of the Agreement will still be valid. This prevents one bad provision from undoing an otherwise good agreement. What's an example of a bad provision, you ask? One example I can think of is a Separation Agreement where the parties base their division of assets on the result of a mathematical error. One party may catch the error and ask the court to amend that specific portion. This clause would prevent the entire agreement from going up on smoke over one innocent error.
- STATEMENT OF UNDERSTANDING. This provision says you understand you had the right to go to trial but instead you determined it was in your best interest to settle; that you read and understand each provision of the Separation Agreement; and that you had the opportunity to have each provision explained to you by an attorney of your choice (and maybe you chose not to hire one).

» RIGHT TO PRIVACY. This provision states you both agree to live separately and not harass the other person.
» ATTORNEY FEES. This provision allocates attorney fees for the end of the case, and for future disputes, and may contain a prevailing party clause, which you need to pay attention to. A prevailing party clause says if there is a dispute in the future, the losing party has to pay the winner's attorney fees.
» INDEMNIFICATION. This provision says if one party breaches the agreement, and the court agrees they breached, they have to pay the fees of the innocent party. Likewise, it also may say if you accuse the other party of breaching the agreement and the court finds they did not breach, you have to pay their attorney fees.
» MEDIATION. This provision may say that if a dispute arises later, you agree to mediate the dispute before filing anything in court.

Although these are what I call "standard" contract provisions, that does not mean they are non-negotiable. For example, I do not believe I ever had anyone request we change the Governing Law provision, but that does not mean I could not have pushed back on it if I had a case where I knew both parties intended to relocate to Arizona and not return to Colorado. If that were the case, we may have put in that the parties intend to both move to Arizona and wish to have Arizona law apply to any future disputes.

When reviewing these, just make sure they apply equally to both parties (instead of, for example, the attorney fee and indemnification portions only punishing you) and that time limits are reasonable to both of you. Also, carefully read the mediation provision wording because this can be abused by hold-out parties who refuse to ever set mediation. You may want to add language to this preventing one person from being able to hold you hostage forever in a requirement to mediate first.

AFFIDAVIT FOR DECREE WITHOUT APPEARANCE

This form is submitted in only pre-decree divorce or legal separation cases.

The Affidavit for Decree without Appearance of Parties is JDF 1201. You can fill out this form to request the Court to grant your divorce or legal separation without making you and the other party appear in court for a final uncontested hearing. Not everyone qualifies for this. Here are the criteria you must meet to qualify:

If one or both of you are *pro se*:

- There are no minor children;
- The wife is not pregnant;
- At the start of the case, the Respondent was served property, or a Co-Petition was filed;
- There are no disputed issues;
- There is no marital property to be divided OR you have entered into an agreement for division of property.

If you are both represented by counsel:

- There are no children OR there are children, but the parties entered into a parenting plan resolving APR;
- The wife is not pregnant OR Wife is pregnant, but the parties entered into a parenting plan resolving APR;
- At the start of the case, the Respondent was served property, or a Co-Petition was filed;

- There are no disputed issues;
- There is no marital property to be divided OR you have entered into an agreement for division of property.

Legal authority allowing entry of decree without appearance can be found at § 14-10-120.3, C.R.S.

PROPOSED DECREE

This form is submitted in only pre-decree divorce or legal separation cases.

The Proposed Decree is JDF 1116. This will become your divorce decree. The Court prefers parties complete the caption and submit it with the other final paperwork.

PROPOSED SUPPORT ORDER

This form is submitted in pre- and post-decree cases involving maintenance or child support.

The Support Order is JDF 1117. The Court prefers parties complete the caption and as much of the form as they are able based on the maintenance and/or child support calculation worksheets and submit it with the other final paperwork.

SECTION 4: POST-TRIAL

CHAPTER 12: POST-TRIAL CHECKLIST

When your case resolves, you must make sure you do what you were ordered to do under your Parenting Plan, Separation Agreement or Permanent Orders. Here is a checklist to help you out.

» Review your orders thoroughly and highlight everything you are required to do.

» Make a list and calendar your deadlines with advance reminders to ensure you are not in contempt. Some of these things may include:

- Transfer title to vehicles.
- Exchange the last of personal property.
- Remove the ex's name from loans; refinance cars and home.
- Have a Quit Claim Deed prepared to transfer home title. I recommend paying an attorney for an hour of time to ensure this is prepared accurately.
- Hire a QDRO preparer to complete transfers of retirement assets. Retirement assets are divvied up by **QDRO** (Qualified Domestic Relations Order). A QDRO is a document that tells the retirement plan administrator that you got divorced, and that the ex gets some portion of the asset. You might need a professional QDRO preparer to prepare your QDRO, although some plan administrators have forms you can fill out and submit with a certified copy of your decree.
- File paperwork to transfer PERA. ***This must be done within 90 days of the date of decree or PERA will deny the transfer, no matter what your order says! See § 14-10-113, C.R.S. Ensure you do this on time!***

Because emotions are high and tempers may be hot after a

your case ends, you do not want to give your ex a reason to file contempt against you, so I strongly recommend ensuring you meet all the required timelines per your court orders so you can finally be done and move on with your fabulous life.

CONCLUSION

I hope this book was helpful to you in this tough time of your life. I am truly sorry that you are having to go through your case, and I wish you the best of luck in the process and the outcome. I hope after this process you are able to successfully coparent your children and that you find peace.

I welcome any feedback you have regarding what I could add to the next edition of this book to make it even more helpful to others going through the process, or regarding any advice you have for those going through it, such as what you wish you had known. You can email me directly at familylawbootcamp@gmail.com.

Thank you for allowing me to assist you with this book. I leave you with advice from legal practitioners.

ADVICE FROM THE BAR

My advice to someone who is trying to draft his or her own separation agreement is to have an objective person with business experience read it after the *pro se* litigant has prepared it. The person to consult would have to be objective (stay away from family members) and have a good business sense. The same holds true for drafting a parenting plan. Have an objective person read it, Again, stay away from family members. Maybe a school counselor or teacher. F. Tezak, Attorney in Littleton, CO.

Be sure to have deadlines for transfers of titles, possessions and bank accounts, for example, within 90 days of the date of decree so that there is a deadline, and nothing is drug out. Be sure to get off any loans if you are not receiving the property. Title is one thing. Being on a mortgage where you are not on the title is absolutely not recommended. The house could be sold without your knowledge or you could be on a loan forever. T. Harrington, Denver Attorney and Mediator.

I think the successful agreements are in the details. For instance, if you are agreeing for one party to keep the marital home and it is jointly titled, is there a provision in your agreement as to when that party will either refinance or sell the home to remove the other party from this financial obligation? Even if you think you and the other party will agree on the details of parenting time later, put those details into your Parenting Plan. The goal is to effectively co-parent; however, the parenting plan will be the default agreement if you disagree later. Teresa Wilkins, Attorney in Englewood, CO.

I tried a very contentious permanent orders hearing in the Arapahoe County District Court. I represented a long-time life insurance salesman. Good catholic. Six kids. After the trial, my client kept all of his life insurance policies. Five or six of them. I remember vividly walking out of the Court telling my client to change the beneficiaries from the now ex-wife to the six children. I saw my client about two weeks later. Again, I asked "Joe did you change the beneficiaries from your ex to the kids?" "Oh, yes" he says. Well, the next week Joe dies of a heart attack while walking out of Sunday mass. He did not change the beneficiary. His kids call me. Three of them are in college and need tuition money. Guess what? Mom would not give them a dime. Attorney in Littleton, CO.

Call the judge Your Honor. Not “ma’am” or “sir.” Attorney in Lone Tree.

Stand up when you talk to the judge every time. Every. Time. Show respect. You want the judge to like you. Judge in Douglas County.

Do not personally attack the other party or the other party’s lawyer. The judge will just think you’re bitter. The judge will not take it to heart. Judge in Douglas County.

Be as nice to the attorney cross examining you as you are to your own lawyer. If you are rude when you are being cross examined, it takes away from your own credibility and the judge thinks you have something to hide. Judge in Arapahoe County.

Don’t use the word “clearly” in arguments, motions, or ever. (e.g., “the law clearly states ____.” Or “this was clearly a denial of my parenting time.” When parties use “clearly” to argue a point, it’s because their point is not “clear.” It weakens your argument. As Shakespeare said, “methinks thou doth protest too much.” Argue your point without rhetoric and it will be stronger. Attorney in Denver.

APPENDIX

Free Legal Resources:

- BACKGROUND CHECKS
- https://cocourts.com/cocourts/. At last check, cost was $7.00
- https://www.cbirecordscheck.com/. At last check, cost was about $6.50.
- **CFI LIST**: https://www.courts.state.co.us/Administration/Division.cfm?Division=pa
- **COURT APPOINTED COUNSEL**
- for extreme risk protection order cases: https://www.courts.state.co.us/Administration/Unit.cfm?Unit=ExtRisk
- all other case types: https://www.courts.state.co.us/Administration/Unit.cfm?Unit=crtappcou
- **COURT RESOURCES**:
- https://www.courts.state.co.us/Administration/Division.cfm?Division=pa
- **COURT WEBSITE**. https://www.courts.state.co.us/.
- For forms, go to https://www.courts.state.co.us/Self_Help/Index.cfm. These sections also have instructions on what forms to complete for many types of cases.
- **GOOGLE SCHOLAR** is a great resource for finding case law for free.
- **LAW SCHOOL LAW LIBRARIES** are great resources to research laws, find laws that apply, put your case into issues. You can ask a law librarian for assistance finding what you need.
- **LEGAL AID CLINICS** are a great resource to talk to an actual lawyer and get guidance on the specific facts of your case. They can help you with figuring out deadlines, calendaring deadlines, disclosure rules, finding law to support your case, and most anything else you need help with. Call your local district court to find out what days the legal aid clinics are held in

your district.

- **LEXIS ADVANCE COLORADO LEGAL RESOURCES** provides free access to Colorado statutes, Colorado Constitution, and court rules.
- **MEDIATORS**: https://www.courts.state.co.us/Administration/Division.cfm?Division=pa
- **METRO VOLUNTEER LAWYERS** is an arm of the Denver Bar Association which matches pro se parties who qualify with volunteer attorneys to represent them in many types of cases including Family law. https://www.denbar.org/mvl
- **SRLOCs** (Self Represented Litigant Coordinator), pronounced "Sherlocks," are attorneys employed by the court to assist self-represented litigants in the effective and efficient processing of court cases while educating them on court statutes, rules, policies, and procedures to help ensure they handle cases properly and expeditiously.

ABOUT THE AUTHOR

Alisha Taibo Coombe has practiced Family Law in Colorado for over ten years. Throughout her career, Alisha has been passionate about using her legal knowledge to serve the community and expand access to justice. Alisha has volunteered in legal aid clinics of all types along the front range and has been a regular volunteer on KUSA Channel 9 Law Line. Alisha chaired the Family Law Pro Se Clinic and currently serves on the Access to Justice Committee and Community Services Committee of the Arapahoe County Bar Association. Alisha is dedicated to helping victims of domestic violence and previously served on the Board of Directors at Gateway Domestic Violence Services. Alisha proposed a simplified family law procedure to the Colorado Supreme Court Standing Committee on Family Justice in order to simplify the process of a family law case for the benefit of those who cannot afford attorneys. Her idea is currently being developed with the assistance of a committee formed specifically for this purpose. Alisha is a proud U.S. Army veteran.

Made in United States
North Haven, CT
10 November 2026

22106122R00115